Cover photograph: "Christ in the City" ©2003
Rev. Sidney Flack, All Rights Reserved.

Rev. Sidney Flack is a pastor of the Evangelical Lutheran Church in America and a fine art photographer. Ordained in 1985, he has served as a missionary in Madagascar and as parish pastor in Kansas, Iowa, and Oklahoma. Rev. Flack has taken pictures most of his life but has been making fine photographs since 1995. His working camera at the time of this publication is a Linhof Technika 4x5 field camera built in 1943. He uses only Kodak 100 TMax film.

Rev. Flack is a Zone System practitioner and prints his negatives by hand on fiber-based papers to current archival standards. Many of Rev. Flack's photographs may be seen and purchased from his website: http://www.divinelightphotography.com. He is represented by the Floating World and M.A. Doran Galleries in Tulsa, Oklahoma.

ഇറ

Fifty per cent of the net proceeds of this book will be donated to Trinity Ministries, a Lutheran nonprofit organization supported by the seven Lutheran congregations of the Tulsa area. Areas of ministry include senior housing, youth ministry, and fellowship between Lutherans and their community. Remaining proceeds will be donated to Partners in Mission, a ministry to the Evangelical Lutheran Church in Guyana, South America, which is coordinated by Fellowship Lutheran Church in Tulsa, Oklahoma.

Human Spirit, Holy Spirit:
Inspirational Stories of Faith Active in Work

ℰℭ

by Fellowship, Ink

Janice Airhart
Michele Fox
Cynthia Gustavson
Linda Holeman
Patti Schmigle

ℰℭ

Printed by Press Group
Tulsa, Oklahoma
November, 2004

Contents

Foreword

ഇൗരു

Human Spirit, Holy Spirit: the two go together. As I read these *Inspirational Stories of Faith Active in Work*, I kept thinking about something that theologian Jürgen Moltmann wrote,

> *The sending of the Holy Spirit is the revelation of God's indestructible affirmation of life and his marvelous joy in life. Where Jesus is, there is life… Where Jesus is, sick people are healed, sad people are comforted, marginalized people are accepted, and the demons of death are driven out. Where the Holy Spirit is present there is life.* (The Source of Life: *The Holy Spirit and the Theology of Life*. Minneapolis: Augsburg Fortress, 1997, p. 19.)

These wonderful stories are about ordinary people, followers of Jesus and members of the body of Christ, in whom and through whom Jesus is giving life to the world. These stories are about ordinary people who serve in the fields of counseling, social work, psychology, family therapy, psychiatry and medicine. Each one, in his or her own way, is using the gifts the Holy Spirit has given to fulfill the vocation given in Holy Baptism, *"to serve all people following the example of the Lord Jesus."*

Five women, who are members of Fellowship Lutheran Church, Tulsa, Oklahoma, interviewed 15 professionals and wrote these stories. "Fellowship, Ink" is the name they chose for their group, but their individual names are also important: Janice Airhart, Michele Fox, Cynthia Gustavson, Linda Holeman, and Patti Schmigle.

Fellowship Lutheran Church has a significant number of people in the healing professions. On a morning walk in the fall of 2002, it dawned on Cynthia Gustavon, a poet and a therapist herself, that it would be interesting to interview some of these professionals, as well as others in area Lutheran congregations. She wondered how their faith impacts the healing work they do. She was aware that other members of Fellowship, like herself, had an interest in and gifts for writing. It wasn't long before these five women were meeting together, brainstorming, writing, and encouraging one another with this project.

> *As I read* Human Spirit, Holy Spirit, *I was moved and inspired by the way those who were interviewed use their gifts in such unselfconscious ways to help and serve others.*

The stories of the healing professionals collected in this volume, as well as the formation of Fellowship, Ink, serve to remind all of us of something that Martin Luther highlighted in his writings. Luther often emphasized that God calls persons through the Holy Spirit to a life of forgiveness and fellowship in the Church and to a life of loving service in all human relationships. It's about using the gifts the Spirit has given us to serve the world that God loves.

As I read *Human Spirit, Holy Spirit*, I was moved and inspired by the way those who were interviewed use their gifts in such unselfconscious ways to help and serve others. They are not only models of faithful service but also humility. Fellowship, Ink has provided a very helpful resource not only for personal inspiration and edification, such as I experienced, but also for small discussion groups in congregations or homes.

I hope that this helpful volume will be a catalyst for all who read and discuss it to reflect on their own gifts and how the Holy Spirit works in and through them to bring life to others and to the world. Reading this volume has inspired me to do more to encourage pastors and congregations to give opportunities for members to share their own stories of how faith impacts what they do in daily life. Reading this volume has also inspired me to encourage church leaders to lift up and to affirm the vocation of all the baptized in their daily lives.

When Fellowship, Ink began this endeavor, the group decided that it would be a non-profit project. Any net proceeds would be shared with Trinity Ministries (50%), a cooperative venture among Tulsa area congregations of the Evangelical Lutheran Church in America, and other projects of Fellowship Lutheran Church (50%). Thank you, Fellowship, Ink, not only for sharing these inspirational stories, but also for your commitment to the mission of the *Holy Spirit* in and through the *Human Spirit.*

Floyd M. Schoenhals, Bishop
Arkansas-Oklahoma Synod, ELCA

Introduction

ഗ∞

The link between faith and physical well-being has been widely reported in recent years, including in the September, 1999 issue of *The Lutheran* ("The Faith Factor" by Melody Hall Blobaum). In a 2002 article in the *International Journal of Psychiatry in Medicine* entitled "Is Depressed Affect a Function of One's Relationship with God?" Dr. Jeff Levin—who pioneered the concept of a faith/health link, beginning in the 1980s—proposed that spiritual beliefs also affect mental health. Jewish psychiatrist Abraham Twerski asserts in his 2000 book, *The Spiritual Self*, "spirituality is central to emotional and mental health, and is key to being truly and profoundly human."

Drawing on such anecdotal and empirical reports, a group of five writers at Fellowship Lutheran Church in Tulsa (known as Fellowship, Ink) initiated a project in 2002 to interview 15 mental health professionals in the Tulsa Lutheran community. What we discovered reinforces the notion that belief in God affects a person's mental and emotional well-being. We also found that spiritual beliefs affect the way practitioners approach their work, even when those they treat or serve don't know the practitioner

8

is a person of faith. For our interview subjects, restoring wholeness among God's people—one by one—is truly an opportunity to follow in Christ's footsteps.

We chose a broad range of practitioners for interview, including psychiatrists, family therapists, social workers, psychologists, a pediatrician, and a genetics counselor. Each of them has served a unique population, and as a result, provided us with a variety of perspectives. All practitioners were asked a list of uniform questions (see page 132), but each discussion suggested its own questions as well. While those we interviewed were Lutheran Christians, we believe that similar dynamics would affect the work of any practitioner for whom spiritual faith is integral to their lives.

As we talked with our interview subjects, one significant point emerged: most practitioners are not free to discuss their faith with clients or patients. For many, ethical codes prescribed by their professions forbid it. For others, employers discourage such discussions. Notable exceptions were those who perform Christian counseling— their clients presumably choose these professionals because they *are* Christian. We discovered, however, that in spite of the restraints that exist for some, every practitioner we interviewed is influenced in some way by his or her faith when dealing with clients or patients. It's clear that it isn't possible to fully compartmentalize our faith lives and our work lives.

For those we interviewed, allowing faith to influence their work is complicated by the vulnerability of those they serve. All were insistent about their obligation to not use their positions of relative authority to proselytize, but all also recognized that personal beliefs affect their actions and how they relate to their clients or patients.

We realize that we—and you—have opportunities to serve others in our workplaces, too. Whether we are writers, plumbers, teachers, managers, cashiers or sales clerks, we face daily issues of integrating our faith into our work. How? When? Choosing if or when to speak about our beliefs in our workplaces is precarious. Our experience in gathering material for this book has given us a renewed respect for the difficulties faced by ordinary Christians as they live out their faiths.

Human Spirit, Holy Spirit: Inspirational Stories of Faith Active in Work tells not only stories of healing, but also stories of Christian healers who are encouraged in the ministry of their daily work by the power of faith. Preceding each chapter is a brief biography of the professional featured in the chapter, and following each are a few questions that might be useful for a study or discussion group.

The writers of Fellowship, Ink were inspired by those whose stories we tell here, and we wish to thank them for sharing such deeply felt stories about their work and those they serve. Without their stories, this book could not have been written.

There are also many others who supported and encouraged us along the way—primarily our families, but also the members of Fellowship Lutheran Church in Tulsa and Pastor Alan Fox. We are grateful to Pastor Sidney Flack for his contribution of the beautiful photograph that adorns the book's cover. Thanks also to Paul Grundmann for the practitioner photos. Betsy Thompson and Leonard Flachman, of Kirk House Publishers, provided editorial feedback that proved helpful. We also are very grateful to Reverend Floyd Schoenhals, bishop of the Arkansas-Oklahoma Synod of the ELCA, for his willingness to provide the Foreword.

May each of you be inspired to seek your own opportunities for faith active in work!

Fellowship, Ink
June, 2004

Dr. Ed Gustavson

Edward Gustavson graduated *summa cum laude* from Gustavus Adolphus College, St. Peter, MN, 1966, and Harvard Medical School, Boston, MA, 1970. His pediatric internship and residency were done at the University of Minnesota, 1970 –73. After a tour of duty as a Major in the U.S. Army from 1973-75 (Tripler Army Hospital, HI,) he was chosen to be a Robert Wood Johnson Clinical Scholar at the Univ. of NC, studying developmental and community pediatrics. He completed a residency in neonatology from the University of Minnesota in 1979. Board certified in both pediatrics and neonatology/perinatology, he has been on the medical school faculty of LA State University, University of MN, and University of OK, as well as medical director of the Children's Justice Center, Tulsa.

Gustavson is currently Director of Pediatrics at Children's Medical Center, Tulsa, OK. He has lectured widely and is the author of numerous medical articles in the area of "failure to thrive" and child neglect, in journals *Teratology, Southern Society For Pediatric Research, American Journal of Diseases of Children, Archives of Pediatrics and Adolescent Medicine, Pediatrics in Review* and in the American Academy of Pediatrics 1994 book, *A Physician's Guide to References and Resources in Child Abuse and Neglect.*

A native of Chicago, IL, he now lives with his wife of 35 years, Cynthia, in Tulsa, OK. They have two children, Britta, 32, and Kent, 25. He is on the advisory board of the Parent Child Center in Tulsa, and a member of Fellowship Lutheran Church.

In The Beginning

෨Ӝ

*Abraham was a hundred years old when his son Isaac was born
to him. And Sarah said, "Who would ever have said to Abraham
that Sarah would nurse children? Yet I have born him a son in
his old age." (Genesis 21: 5-9)*

*And she gave birth to her firstborn son and wrapped him in
bands of cloth, and laid him in a manger, because there was no
room for them in the inn." (Luke 2: 7)*

An African-American mother from rural
Louisiana had delivered her baby suddenly
and unexpectedly three months early. She
was a teacher's aide who had worked in a small country
schoolhouse. According to Ed Gustavson, her doctor, "Her
baby was born with life's breath, but gradually fluid filled
his lungs." On the third day it was evident that her hopes
and prayers for the little one she could hardly touch were
futile. "She explained to me, with tears in her eyes, which
brought tears to me also, that I didn't need to worry. She
said, 'Jesus has my baby and me in his arms.' There was no
hesitation in her voice despite the tears. All of the complex
discussions, which I'd learned to make during my years

of training, paled in comparison. This woman understood the Christian life. Then she said, 'Just put him in my arms.' And so I disconnected the wires and tubes of the respirator and put him into her arms to die."

"That's how I learned to do it," says Gustavson. "In those days it was unheard of to let babies die in their mother's arms. Nurses, doctors, hospital administrators questioned me, but I had been shown the way Jesus would have done it, and so, after that, if the parents wished it, I allowed their infant to die in its mother's arms. After all, it was just sustaining the bond that God began in pregnancy, continued throughout the birth process, and fulfilled in its precious time on earth."

> *"This woman exhibited a great reverence for life and death. She demonstrated to me God's healing power of spirit."*

Gustavson has witnessed the spirituality of the mother/infant bond in death as well as in new life. He has been at the birth and death of countless premature and developmentally disabled infants. He states, "Mothers and infants are inseparably united, and thus, when an infant dies, so does a part of the mother."

The birth, described above, was one of his first infant deaths as a young doctor in Shreveport, Louisiana. As he related the story, his voice wavered, and he stopped a moment. He said, "It's been over 20 years, and I still remember it plainly. This woman exhibited a great reverence for life and death. She demonstrated to me God's healing power of spirit."

As a developmental pediatrician and neonatologist, Gustavson has vast experience in addressing the spiritual and emotional needs of infants and parents. He explains that newborns are wholly dependent on their caregivers, usually their mothers, for food, clothing, shelter, and also for the other ways that mothers show love, such as by touch, verbal communication, and body language. "We know from studies of children during war, and children raised in institutions, that a child who is fed and clothed, but not touched, will die. Infants are totally self-absorbed, totally parasitic on their host, and yet, are still created in the image of God. This living in complete dependence is based on trust. The noted psychiatrist, Erik Erikson, taught us that the developmental task of the infant is to develop trust and if that trust is broken, or never developed, the child will grow into an adult who trusts no one."

Gustavson believes that the art of medicine is a combination of spirituality, science and psychology. But he states that "psychology" is a bad word to use in this case because it often suggests dualistic body/mind thinking. "When working in a meaningful medical situation, the intimacy surpasses just cognition or just emotion. It requires a wholistic view of the patient's life and surroundings."

Gustavson chuckles and then adds, "The only 'psychology' of infancy is in the development of trust." He explains that the ability to think is limited because the baby's brain frontal lobe is not yet in use. When adults misperceive infants in terms of psychology and informed decision making, as if infants cried just to make them mad, then the infant is at risk for abuse. This is a breach of trust. Babies are not psychological beings, they are spiritual beings surviving by the grace of God and parents.

Gustavson cites a book by Jewish theologian, Martin Buber, called *I and Thou*. In it Buber described two kinds of relationships, "I and thou," and "I and it." The "I and thou" relationship mirrors the connection of God to humans. In Christianity we see this when Jesus calls God "Abba," which is close to our English word "Daddy." This relationship is intimate and loving. The opposite is an "I and it" relationship, which treats humans in terms of what they can do for us, and which lacks a spiritual bond.

The infant-maternal bond, Gustavson feels, is an "I and thou" relationship. This bond is intimate, loving and spiritual in nature, and allows parents to survive the dirty diapers, the middle-of-the-night screams, and the constant attending to this new family addition. The only reward for all this care is in the eye contact, the occasional smile, and the wonderful feeling that floods parent's hearts. If for some reason a mother or caregiver develops an "I and it" relationship with her infant, then that child is at risk for neglect or abuse.

In the world of Jesus, children had to grow up quickly. But he talked tenderly about them. Not only did he talk about protecting and nurturing the little children, he also referred many times to the good shepherd watching carefully over his sheep.

In our modern world we describe this spiritual relationship as "bonding," or "mother-infant attachment." Gustavson adds that we also now know that it is hard-wired into the normal mother's biochemistry. The chemical HCG, which increases in amount and prepares the womb for pregnancy, in combination with oxytocin, biologically programs the mother's attention to her infant. That infant bond, which is formed in the first moments of life, will change the mother's behavior toward her child permanently. Mothers who are not awake during the birth process or who are separated for health reasons; fathers and other family members or friends; or adoptive parents can spiritually bond to their babies through loving and attending to them, even though they do not have the powerful chemical incentive for bonding.

Gustavson's language switches from "scientist" to "believer" as he states, "Anything which disrupts this bonding process acts in opposition to the gospel's intent, that to love is the greatest commandment."

For the newborn everything (including the infant's own hand) is a foreign object, and he/she has no understanding of the difference between self and non-self: the infant is at one with its mother, not realizing they are separate individuals. He/she sees only in black and white and in patterns, and the complex understanding of object/ground appears much later. Feelings are clearly present at first, but they are simple. They are either present or absent. The infant's survival mechanism is adaptive, or maladaptive. As for the infant's cognition, its ability to think, it is polar rather than multi-faceted. The newborn cannot tell one human face from another in the first months. When Baby starts crying as Mother leaves, the infant has reached a developmental milestone.

It is easy to see the infant is totally dependent, and the mother, father, or caregiver must put aside their own self-interest in the interest of their child. In Christianity we call this "agape" love, the love God shows all God's children. God's gift given to us in our biochemistry, to physically bond, and the gift given us in our hearts, to spiritually bond, is truly the gift of love.

Gustavson is a doctor who knows the science of keeping newborns healthy. He knows too that science points to the importance of not-so-easily measured variables in the life of an infant, such as the infant/mother bond, which he believes mirrors the God/human bond. He practices medicine with an understanding of the wholeness of mind and body, spirit and psyche, and believes that we are complex human organisms held lovingly "in the arms of Jesus."

₨‑⊳

Questions:

1. Sarah and Mary both praised God for the birth of their children. They also acknowledged surprise at their great joy. If you are a parent, or aunt or uncle, how did you feel at the birth of your child? What new things did you discover? How did you praise God?

2. Did your joy become frustration, exhaustion, when you realized how dependant your infant was? Gustavson uses the term "parasitic" to describe a child's dependence, yet also calls children "created in the image of God." How do parents balance that tension?

3. Discuss the difference between "I-Thou" and "I-It," Buber's terms to describe relationships. How do those terms relate to family, co-workers, other Christians, non-Christians, non-Americans, and "enemies?" Which term would Jesus use in describing his "enemies?"

4. As a parent, did you feel a bond with your infant? Did it last as the child grew older? How is that bond different from other kinds of relationships, or even other kinds of love, that you have felt?

5. What does it mean to be "held lovingly in the arms of Jesus?"

Dr. Terese Hall

Terese Hall holds an M.A. in Christian Counseling and a Ph.D. in Clinical Psychology. Her doctoral dissertation, entitled "Functions of Religious and Non-religious Coping," is currently being reviewed for publication. She is also a lawyer and holds a J.D. from the University of Oklahoma.

Hall works today as a self-employed psychologist with a clinical and a forensic practice. Besides her freelance work, Hall teaches psychology at Oral Roberts University. She is a member of Fellowship Lutheran Church, where she and her husband Ed Decker are employed as directors of the Pastoral Care ministry.

Within the Christian counseling field, Hall has been published in the *Journal of Psychology and Christianity* and in the *Journal of Psychology and Theology*. Her essay, "Pastoral Care of Women," was included as a chapter in the book *Soul Care: Pentecostal Character Perspectives*. She's very interested in research and writing about women's spiritual development. Hall is a member of the American Psychological Association and the Oklahoma Bar Association. Additionally, she is a member of the Christian Association for Psychological Studies (CAPS), where she is currently serving as President of the Southwest Regional Board.

Hall and her husband reside in Tulsa. She is mother to Amanda, Sarah, and David, and grandmother to two small boys. In her spare time, Hall enjoys reading, writing, hiking, fishing, and traveling. It is her family, though, that holds the key to her heart. For as Hall proudly proclaims, "I love my grandkids!"

Real Freedom

ഇ൭൪൫

*Dinah, the daughter whom Leah had borne to Jacob, went out
to visit the women of the country, and Shechem, son of Hamor
the Hivite the local prince, saw her; he took her, lay with her
and dishonoured her. But he remained true to Jacob's daughter
Dinah; He loved the girl and comforted her. So Shechem said
to his father Hamor, 'Get me this girl for a wife.' When Jacob
heard that Shechem had violated his daughter Dinah, his sons
were with the herds in the open country, so he said nothing until
they came home. Meanwhile Shechem's father Hamor came out
to Jacob to discuss it with him. When Jacob's sons came in from
the country and heard, they were grieved and angry, because in
lying with Jacob's daughter he had done what the Israelites held
to be an outrage, an intolerable thing. (Genesis 34: 1-7, NEB)*

S o begins a rarely heard tale from the Old
Testament. It seems oddly contemporary;
this could have been a news brief pulled from
today's headlines had the names been changed. Later
in the story, it is Dinah's brothers who take revenge on
Shechem for the rape of their sister. The lives of all the
main characters in this story are changed by Shechem's

rash deed. Yet it is Dinah, whose only crime was being a woman and attracting the attention of a man, whose feelings we would want to learn more of. And yet, we are told nothing more of her.

As a counseling therapist in Tulsa, Dr. Terese Hall encounters many abused and emotionally scarred women in her work. Like Dinah, these women were often innocent victims of the abuse they endured. Unlike her, the men that should have done the protecting are often the very ones administering the violence. "Many of my clients feel forgotten or ignored by God," Hall says. She feels it is advantageous to bring her Christian world view to therapy sessions. "There is a lot of suffering out there, and it is important to know God does care." Hall sees her role as encouraging her clients to keep the lines of communication with God open. She says, "I have never been proven wrong on this: God will answer you, if you keep on talking."

"The second thing I can do as a Christian is to provide a physical presence for the duration of the healing process. Many of my patients are women who have been the victims of emotional, sexual, or physical abuse. In most cases, these women suffered for years before seeking help from the outside. Consequently, freeing their current lives from the memories that haunt them is not something that will happen in the space of an hour or two." Hall says, "I believe that it is crucial to take the time needed to enable the patient to learn to use the tools that will promote healing. For many abuse victims, therapy is a matter of years, not weeks or months."

Hall has found that women, in general, tend to be dishonest with themselves about the depth of their anger. Many have suffered abuse at the hands of someone they once loved and trusted. Hall continues, "These women have to learn to set aside their 'good girl' faith before they can begin to have an open line of communication with God."

Just what represents a 'good girl faith?' Hall

tells us, "Instead of fighting back when something hurts them, 'good girls' learn to hide their true feelings. When something hideous is staring them right in the face, they tend to look the other way. They are quiet."

Churches that promote "faith healing," or the belief in miracles of healing where a person's faith is strong, can sometimes present a stumbling block to a person in need of emotional healing. For example, Hall cited an instance where a victim of alcoholism, rape and incest took her problems to another Christian counselor. The woman was told to simply forgive those who had hurt her, and she would be healed. It sounds simple; it even reminds us of Jesus' words on the cross. The only difficulty was that the woman in question was not able to do this. Try as she might, she still harbored angry feelings toward those that hurt her.

Ten years ago, Hall conducted a survey at a women's conference in Tulsa, Oklahoma. She was surprised to learn that as many as two thirds of the women attending were having significant problems with their faith. They claimed their faith actually seemed to make things harder for them in the world. Particularly hard to reconcile were the messages that place women in roles subjective to men, regardless of their abilities. "One woman commented how she seemed to 'catch on' to the teaching in Sunday school faster than the man seated next to her. Yet she felt compelled to sit silent much of the time, because she didn't want to be seen as a domineering, outspoken woman. Apparently, women in our society are hesitant to use the gifts God entrusted to them."

"Apparently, women in our society are hesitant to use the gifts God entrusted to them."

Hall believes that women in America are socialized in a way that robs them of their full potential. She states, "In our culture, women somehow pick up cues that they are to be soft and yielding. Women traditionally become the caregivers and the nurturers in our society. Women predominate in the fields of nursing and office management. They are still primarily responsible for the care and education of our nation's children. All of which are low-paying professions, making it particularly hard for single mothers."

Fortunately, the Gospel of Jesus Christ liberates us by redirecting our focus. Instead of a religion based upon the fulfillment of God's law, Jesus tells us all we really need to do is be baptized and believe in him. Hall was privileged to witness a powerful example of the way a client's faith moved her toward healing. She was working with a woman that was raped by a group of teenaged boys when she was only five years old. As a young child, she didn't understand what the boys were doing to her. In her mind, she was certain they were trying to kill her. This memory had become a real stumbling block for her, in her relationship with God. Hall knew she had to help her client get past this, but the woman seemed unable to move on. Here is how she describes the healing that took place.

"I said to her, 'I don't know what else we can say about this. Shall we pray?' When we began to pray together, the rape scene again appeared in the woman's mind. She began crying, and she witnessed once again the whole ugly scene. Only this time, she saw Jesus there, watching what the boys were doing to her. And he was very angry at what was happening. He was also crying. He stayed with her the whole time. It was God that really led her through this; I was just helping. It was just incredible."

Hall concluded with this: "If we look at Jesus, he was such a radical feminist. Because of His love for us, Christianity holds real promise and real freedom for us all."

ഇരു

Questions:

1. How have society's viewpoints regarding race and gender affected you in your dreams for a happier life?
2. Have you ever experienced judgment from Christian brothers and sisters, when you felt you were following God's plan?
3. Have you ever had a hard time freeing yourself from painful memories? Reflect upon how these memories stifle your growth, and consider yielding them to God in prayer, perhaps with the help of a trusted friend or confidant.

Dr. Carolyn Ekenstam

Dr. Carolyn Ekenstam sees her work as a prison psychologist as an opportunity to hear others' life and faith stories and to respond to their faith questions. "I can also provide an example of someone caring in a mostly non-caring place."

Ekenstam received a B.S. degree from Texas Lutheran University in 1966, but was driven to pursue a second bachelor's degree in psychology in 1990, after the death of her son Erik. She eventually received her Ph.D. from The University of Tulsa in 1997 and has served as prison psychologist at Dick Connor Correctional Facility in Hominy, Oklahoma for five years.

Ekenstam's dissertation research led to publication of the article "Coercion and the Outcome of Psychiatric Hospitalization" in the *International Journal of Law and Psychiatry*. She also wrote an article for the *ELCA Family Resource Series* called "Ministry with Families after Suicide." She is a member of the American Psychological Association, the American Psychology – Law Society, and the Christian Association for Psychological Studies. Ekenstam lives in Cleveland, Oklahoma and attends Fellowship Lutheran Church. She has a grown daughter, Karla.

When she's not working, Ekenstam enjoys reading, playing games with friends, exploring Oklahoma and traveling. She also volunteers in several capacities at her church.

Building Trust Behind Bars

ಐಂಞ

Make me to know your ways, O Lord;
teach me your paths.
Lead me in your truth, and teach me,
for you are the God of my salvation;
for you I wait all day long.
Be mindful of your mercy, O Lord,
and of your steadfast love,
for they have been from of old.
Do not remember the sins of my youth or my transgressions;
according to your steadfast love remember me,
for your goodness' sake, O Lord! (Psalm 25: 4-7)

"Sometimes they tell me their stories to shock me, and I *am* shocked, but not so much by the stories. I'm shocked that they're willing to tell them to me," Dr. Carolyn Ekenstam says about the inmates in the men's correctional facility where she serves as prison psychologist. "Usually, they're looking to see if I can be trusted with the ugly truth about them. Some are looking for absolution, but sometimes they just need to get their stories told. I sometimes sense that they're afraid I'll think they're monsters, but ironically, I'm more hopeful of

27

their chances for change if they have those fears. The ones I worry about are the ones who try to impress me with the horrific details of their crimes."

Not all the prisoners Ekenstam works with have horrific stories to tell, but those convicted of violent crimes are a special challenge. One inmate Ekenstam described as a "bad guy, even scary," who had been at the prison a short time named her the beneficiary of a life insurance policy and asked her if he could pray for her and her work. He was in a lock-down unit at the time, Ekenstam says, and rather than holding hands as they would have liked, both held onto the door while he prayed for her. Though she was at first uncomfortable with the request, Ekenstam says, "It felt really good to have him pray for me. Later, when he was being transferred to another facility, he asked me to call his mother from time to time to check on how he was doing. This was a guy who a few weeks before had been banging on the door. One of my male colleagues who was down there was afraid he might come after him."

Ekenstam isn't any more surprised by an inmate's request to pray for her than she is by an inmate's confession. Inside prison walls, where a variety of religious groups regularly evangelize and a nondenominational chapel is just down the hall, finding God is a relatively common experience. But as one inmate who was incarcerated for the third time told Ekenstam, "I need to remember to take God out the gate with me."

"What happens so much of the time is that inmates end up going back to the environment that landed them in jail in the first place," Ekenstam says. "When they get out of jail, if they can't find jobs, they go back to doing what they know." That often includes stealing or selling drugs.

The prison population is one in which spirituality, religion, and scriptures are regularly discussed during psychotherapy sessions. For Ekenstam, who completed her Ph.D. program in psychology at The University of Tulsa in 1997, where it was made clear that spirituality had no place in the practice of psychology, that has meant some adjustment in her expectations. It's an adjustment she was happy to make.

Some of her training was completed at Eastern State Hospital in Vinita, Oklahoma, where she witnessed firsthand the effects of the closure of many local and regional mental health facilities. Many of her patients there were suicidal or suffered serious mental disorders, some of which featured religious delusions. When they can no longer get the medical care they need in their communities, some of those with severe disorders take drastic measures. "They have to go somewhere," Ekenstam says. Many end up in the penal system.

Ekenstam reviews all inmates who enter the facility and schedules ongoing sessions, usually on a monthly basis, with those who are prescribed psychotropic medications. Some others with milder disorders, she sees less frequently. It's risky for an inmate to be seen by the prison psychologist, she says. "There's a real stigma attached to it, and the inmates tease each other about it." That's why Ekenstam leaves it to her clients to bring up discussions involving faith.

"It's risky for an inmate to be seen by the prison psychologist. There's a real stigma attached to it, and the inmates tease each other about it."

Religious groups also are highly visible inside prison walls, according to Ekenstam, though most of them are literal in theology. That high visibility makes it easy for inmates to discuss religion with her, she says, and she feels she can be helpful by presenting a more tolerant and accepting approach to Christianity. Their discussions usually involve scripture more than prayer. "If I know religion is a piece of them, then I'm more willing to talk about scripture passages or other spiritual or religious issues."

There are several reasons why spiritual issues come up during therapy. Although it's not usually the reason an inmate comes for therapy, a topic that comes up often is a question about moral issues. "A lot of them have issues with sex. In a closed environment, with no good outlet for sexual energy, there are questions about the morality of masturbation, and they want to know how I'm going to deal with it. Am I going to condemn them for asking, for instance? They learn that I'm willing to talk about these things. I'm not averse to asking questions about religion, but sometimes the reason they're coming to me is that they're amenable to change and that has come because they've become a Christian or been saved or baptized. That's part of what they tell me, then."

One thing Ekenstam doesn't do is pray *with* her clients. "It could present problems if the practice were made known among the prisoners. But I do often pray *for* them." Ekenstam is well aware what happens in therapy sessions often becomes public knowledge in the prison, so she is careful to let it be known that although she is a Christian, she respects each prisoner's right to his own beliefs. Her clients include Wiccans, Muslims, Christians, and Native Americans who subscribe to Native American spirituality. The prison accommodates each faith through a chapel in the facility that is used by all on a prearranged schedule.

"Even with those of other faiths, I can use that knowledge to ask them what their faith means for them and how their spiritual beliefs affect their behavior. I'm pretty sensitive to the Islamic community, for instance, that does prayer at two o'clock on Friday afternoons. I don't schedule them for those times." The challenge Ekenstam faces in dealing with some of the male Muslim inmates, however, is their reluctance to listen to a woman. As with most other issues, she meets that one head-on. Those inmates for whom her gender is a problem can choose not to pursue therapy.

That her clients know she is Christian is only part of the story, though, Ekenstam says. "A lot of my clients are most familiar with fundamentalist Christian theology, and the judgmental perspective is sometimes an obstacle in their healing. Some inmates ask for me, whether or not they know I'm Christian, because they know I'm not judgmental."

One inmate came to her with a story of reluctant conversion. "He said he wasn't sure he wanted to change, but it's a God thing. 'Things are changing and I don't quite understand what's happening'," he told her. The prison staff had noted changes in his behavior, but he wasn't aware of them. This created an opportunity for Ekenstam to begin to talk to him in terms of how being a Christian changed his behavior. "I could ask what God would have him do, rather than what he would do. The change has been so rapid, he isn't sure how to deal with it, and that's hurt his healing process. He's finally able to put himself in someone else's place, however, which he couldn't do before." That empathy for others is important to his progress, she says.

Another inmate she worked with became a Christian, but with unrealistic expectations. "When everything didn't go his way when he prayed, he just gave up on prayer, and he got worse. That's an example in which the idea of spirituality was detrimental to his mental health."

Despite occasional setbacks, Ekenstam is convinced that spirituality has a place in mental health healing. "When a client is anti-Christian, I feel like one of the pieces I can use to help them is gone. It's like a three-legged stool. If you take one of the legs away, the stool doesn't work very well, and you're trying to do other things to create that last piece."

For those clients who aren't Christian, Ekenstam respects their decisions, too. She sometimes suggests inmates attend a religious service and sometimes refers inmates to a chaplain, but she respects their right to refuse. She also remains open to the variety of spiritual practices represented within the prison. Native American inmates, about 10 percent of the total population of her facility, are supported more fully in their spiritual practices than others, she believes, because they're part of a smaller community where there is closer relationship between individual members.

For those inmates who are Christian, Ekenstam believes they possess a kind of hope that other inmates don't share. "Their spiritual foundation helps them emotionally and mentally. They're less likely to give up, and I deal with the giving up all the time. Some even come to see prison as their ministry. One gentleman who was incarcerated here briefly for murder was transferred to California, where he continues to write letters to me occasionally. He's become very religious and studies all the time. He asks me why God hasn't let him out of prison. There was a point at which he began to lose hope of being released, and one of his fellow inmates committed suicide. I suggested to him that he view his time in prison as an opportunity to minister to other prisoners. I even quoted a portion of my pastor's sermon to him, in which he said we don't know what the future holds, but we know who holds the future. After that, his letters took on a different tone, and he continues to write to me."

> *"I suggested to him that he view his time in prison as an opportunity to minister to other prisoners."*

Another former client, an inmate transferred to a facility in Stringtown, Oklahoma in the spring of 2003, recently commented to Ekenstam in a letter that readings in the epistles of Peter and John were helpful to him in letting go of past debts he felt were due him. "I should have read the whole Bible by now," he says in the letter. "My aunt gave it to me in December, 1985, but I haven't (read it all). I have read chapters and books in the Old Testament, but not all of it."

After his transfer, he found himself in a cell with none of his possessions; then, a prison ministry volunteer brought him a new Bible. "I did a lot of praying, then He

(God) blessed me with his word. Dr. Ekenstam, I don't know how things are going to go from here, but I want you to know, I am not going to give up. I am trying to do right, and I should've let that debt go a long time ago."

Ekenstam builds the kinds of relationships with her clients that give them hope for a better future and helps them learn to trust others. They recognize there is someone who genuinely cares about them, and for some that is a novel experience. For her part, Ekenstam finds it personally helpful to receive correspondence occasionally that reminds her that her efforts are appreciated.

Though Ekenstam values an inmate's need to tell her his story, some prisoners who choose to discuss religious issues present a different sort of problem. "The guys who have religious delusions pose a dilemma. Some border on normal, but may be ill. How do I know whether they are really communicating with God or suffering delusions?" Ekenstam says she tries to leave room for both, though it's often difficult to believe their messages are from God. "I don't argue or deny that it's a possibility."

About three to five percent of her clients have been diagnosed with schizophrenia, and fifteen percent of the total inmates are on psychotropic medications. Some exhibit dysfunction but don't fit specific mental illness criteria. For others, the line between genuine faith and mental illness is blurred. Inmates sometimes speak to her of visions, but their stories are incomprehensible. One client fears the spirit will come "get him" if he talks about his beliefs to her. Another said God told him to burn down a bar, which Ekenstam finds difficult to believe.

These are the times Ekenstam says she suffers the greatest doubts. "At all times, I treat my clients with respect, but sometimes I can't pay as much heed to what they tell me. Some cases are very complicated."

Practicing psychology behind bars might not seem an attractive environment for many professionals, but Ekenstam clearly feels called to this work. It gives her the opportunity to witness to her Christian faith by remaining open and nonjudgmental about her clients' experiences—both criminal and spiritual.

ഏരു

Questions:

1. Have you ever asked, as the Psalmist did, that God not remember your transgressions? Why is this a timeless and universal human request?
2. What do those who have never been behind bars have in common with inmates who need help "taking God out the gate?" What gates do we face?
3. Who do we turn to for help when we recognize that we are a sinful people, and live "in bondage to sin?" Is this different whether a person is incarcerated or not?
4. What aspects of Dr. Ekenstam's work in the prison are Christian ministry?
5. Why do you think Dr. Ekenstam is able to approach her clients with such compassion?

Marjorie Erdmann

Marjorie Erdmann received her
M.S. in Family Relations and Child
Development: Marriage and Family
Therapy from Oklahoma State
University in 1993. Two of her
primary therapy roles dealt directly
with children and families through
school, where she provided diagnosis,
treatment plans, individual, family
and group therapy. She served
as Director of Day Treatment and
Alternative School Programs in
Pawhuska, Oklahoma, and as School Liaison and Coordinator
of School Outreach. She also served as primary therapist to
Children's Medical Center in Tulsa, handling acute, residential
day treatment for adolescents and children. She was also school
liaison and coordinator of school outreach for art therapy, group
and social work programs.

Erdmann has been a member of Oklahoma Association of Marital
and Family Therapy, and she published an article regarding
Vietnam Veterans Spousal Relations in 1994.

Erdmann has traveled to Guyana three times on missions with
Fellowship Lutheran Church, providing outreach to HIV-AIDS
patients and families. She and her husband Ken have two
children, Mary and Henry. She now focuses her time on her
family, mom's group activities, and watches the dust grow on
her golf clubs.

First Things First

ℬℭ

We are pressed on every side by troubles, but not crushed and broken. We are perplexed because we don't know why things happen as they do, but we don't give up and quit. We are hunted down, but God never abandons us. We get knocked down, but we get up again and keep going. These bodies of ours are constantly facing death just as Jesus did; so it is clear to all that it is only the living Christ within who keeps us safe. (2 Corin. 4: 8-10)

The therapist admired Amos, her creative thirteen-year-old patient, who was at the moment avoiding her gaze. She had just asked how homework was going for him these days, and he was stalling. He finally gave an unexpected response, replying that his grandfather wants him to study more. Intrigued, his therapist asked Amos to tell her more about the conversation. He casually relayed the conversation about his homework and life in general, including his grandfather's advice that only one person can make Amos happy, and that one person is Amos. The therapist nodded, pleased with the sage advice. She smiled at Amos as she tried to recall how many months it had been since the boy's grandfather had passed away.

Marjorie Erdmann never brought spiritual or religious beliefs to her therapy sessions, but sometimes her patients would. "If it's important to them, they'll bring it with them," she says, "and it's important not to get in the way of what they bring in terms of spirituality." She tells of the Native American adolescent who relayed the conversation he had the previous night with his grandfather. She listened intently, knowing that the young man's grandfather had passed away several months earlier. "While I was no expert in Native American spiritual beliefs and practices, through experience I learned that it wasn't uncommon for them to have visits from their relatives who had passed away. To them, it was a sign of peace and comfort, and provided a way of dealing with death. The boy was not delusional, and as a therapist it was important that I was not concerned with whether or not his grandfather actually visited him. Rather, I was interested in what a visit like that would mean to him spiritually and what role that spiritual experience played in either encouraging or impeding his healing. Had I brought my own beliefs to the table in such circumstances, we may have bypassed or even shut down one therapeutic path."

Erdmann spent six years as a marriage and family therapist, helping families through difficult problems. She chose a challenging first assignment as a therapist by accepting a position as program coordinator for the Pawhuska (Oklahoma) Alternative School in 1993. Alternative schools provide a school environment for children with mental and behavioral problems where their academic needs can be met along with family or individual therapy they need. While students have teachers who provide traditional school curriculum, they also are provided with a therapist and time to address their family or personal issues.

Sometimes it's the simple, pragmatic things that

have the most important impact on people's lives. To a child with a serious behavioral disorder, for example, spending a few hours focusing on painting or drawing can provide them with relief from their daily troubles. "It gives those children a sense of normalcy and something positive to talk about when they return to school. Some children with behavioral problems don't have many options when it comes to summer camps and activities other kids their age experience, so talking about how they spent their summer vacation isn't always easy," says Erdmann, who spent two years as a school liaison utilizing art therapy programs with Children's Medical Center in Tulsa. "A simple thing like a summer art camp can mean a lot to these children."

> *Sometimes it's the simple, pragmatic things that have the most important impact on people's lives.*

In discussing the benefits of art therapy, Erdmann recalls something called the "wet room," a place completely lined with tiled walls and floors. Children were allowed to draw or paint on the walls, allowing them to address their issues through art. At the end of the session, the children were required to wash their artwork from the walls. "It was the entire therapeutic process that was important. Washing away what they had expressed in art on the walls allowed them to see that problems can be washed away. Problems don't have to stain us forever," she says.

Erdmann once again emphasizes the importance of addressing what may seem like very basic issues for a patient so that a path for further recovery can be opened. "Family therapy can be hard to come by," Erdman explains. Parents naturally expect some behavioral and social problems as their children become adolescents. But many aren't prepared when problems develop much earlier or become more serious. And families sometimes have trouble determining who to call when problems do surface. They usually begin seeking help from sources within their core circle of influence, starting with family members, then from resources at work or school. They may then look for help from a pastor or someone in their church family, and may ultimately seek help from a mental health professional or therapist.

Erdmann underscores the importance of assessing each patient's resources and helping them get in touch with a resource that provides definable, measurable, tangible, and sustainable support. She explains, "The healing process is about becoming stronger, and resources help people do that. Personal religion and the church community are valid, powerful places for that strength, but are not necessarily required for healing."

"For some, religion and religious practice can be heavy into guilt and shame," says Erdmann. "People don't get better by feeling more guilt and shame than they are already burdened with. It's best to allow the client to decide if their religion will be a part of their healing."

Erdmann describes her first mission trip to Guyana, where she assisted social workers in a gyno-urinary medicine clinic. "The clinic treated women on Mondays, men on Tuesdays, prostitutes on Wednesdays, and homosexuals on Thursdays," she says, providing detail to put into perspective the objective of the clinic and the level of care they were able to provide as therapists. "Your natural inclination as a Christian might be to focus on the broad moral issues, such as how to get the Wednesday patients out of a life of prostitution. But the most important and effective assistance we could provide was focused on much more pragmatic things, like how to deal with the health risks they faced and finding ways for them to make money other than prostitution. The clinic used an empowerment model that focused on creating practical solutions through the personal power of the patient. The intent was to identify what the patients can do to help themselves, and the solutions they developed were very pragmatic. We were there to help them with those basic issues, not to bring the church to the people."

"Christianity takes a leap of faith," Erdmann adds. "It's intangible, elusive and somewhat mystical. There is no laboratory test for Christianity. Unfortunately, for many years mental health had the same aura about it. For that reason, mixing spirituality with therapy can challenge the legitimacy of mental health treatment. With advancements in research and medical technology, though, we now have tangible chemical and behavioral facts to work with. The entire field is much less elusive, and there are more proven methods and treatments."

There is no doubt in Erdmann's mind that spirituality can help in the process of healing, however. It can be very helpful in areas like acceptance and coping. But she reinforces that the choice and origin of that religious resource must come from the client. Christ may be part of the journey, but not exclusive of pharmacologic treatment and therapy.

When asked how she draws upon her own spirituality as a therapist, Erdmann replies, "I've found that I needed to make my church life a safe haven. For a while, I helped with support classes and with needs from the congregation members, but I eventually had to separate the two callings. Church is where and how I get recharged so that I can provide care to others. Counseling is really personal stuff. It's not straightforward issues that can be solved quickly, like ridding a child of a fever. It carries with it things that aren't so easy to let go of at the end of the day." This approach to her own life is further evidence of her seemingly inherent way of sorting through priorities, putting first things first. By addressing their most basic and fundamental issues, her clients could find a way to make that second step to improving their lives.

෫)ର

Questions:

1. How do you use your spiritual beliefs or your church life to help you set priorities? To get recharged for other aspects of your life?
2. Can you think of examples where you've cleared the way to make your life better by addressing the fundamentals first?
3. Have you experienced a situation where you chose to keep your own beliefs or priorities to yourself in order to help someone else? Were you able to do that successfully? Why or why not?
4. 2 Corinthians 4:8-10 reminds us that God never abandons us. How confident are you in times of adversity? What helps you to "get up and keep going?"

Kirstin Magnuson

Kirstin Magnuson is a therapist with Youth and Family Services of Bartlesville, a nonprofit organization that offers counseling to at-risk children and teens and their families. A native of Oshkosh, Wisconsin and a lifelong dancer, she attended the Musical Theater and Dance program at Brigham Young University in Utah. After transferring to Oral Roberts University, she received her Bachelor of Arts in Theology in 2002.  She earned her Master's degree in Christian Counseling from ORU in 2004.

Magnuson is active within Fellowship Lutheran Church in Tulsa, Oklahoma, where her husband, Chad, serves as Youth Director. She regularly leads a small group youth study and plays keyboard for the IGNITION youth service on Sunday nights. A part-time dance instructor, Magnuson also enjoys playing tennis, tossing a football around with her husband, drawing house plans, and watching vintage films featuring Fred Astaire and Ginger Rogers.

Dancing in the Spirit

℘℃

". . . praise him with timbrel and with dance"
(Psalm 150)

Sometimes it's hard to talk about God. All too
often, words used to describe or defend the
Almighty are polarizing and destructive. As
believers on both sides of hot-button issues like choice, gay
marriage, or the separation of church and state will attest,
one carelessly uttered word or phrase has the frightening
power to permanently expose and accentuate the fissures
in belief that might otherwise lie safely dormant.

Perhaps this partly explains the powerful appeal
of dance. Dance is an art form, a sublime blend of grace,
symmetry, rhythm, and power. But it is also a language,
silent and universal, an authentic and primal means of
communication that transcends race, culture, class, and
belief.

Is dance spiritual? Its increasing use as a regular
part of worship in even the most conservative of Christian
congregations, as well as the growing number of dance
companies that celebrate the sacred, suggest dance can

be an important means of honing our connection to spirituality. For the ballerina breathlessly executing a grande jete to the nine-year-old watching raptly from the mezzanine, dance connects the body with the spirit. Dance allows us to retain the sense of wholeness and inclusion that comes from not splitting the body and the spirit apart. Dance also is a celebration of our corporality and consequently a celebration of God's incarnation as Christ.

Kirstin Magnuson is one person for whom spirituality and dance are intertwined. For her, dance is as much a personal meditation as it is a performance, a sacrifice of praise through movement that brings her closer to God. "It's such an important creative outlet for me," she says. "God has blessed me with the means of expressing what's in my heart and sharing that joy with the world."

> *Dance allows us to retain the sense of wholeness and inclusion that comes from not splitting the body and the spirit apart.*

Music and dance have been an integral part of Magnuson's life since childhood. The youngest of three children in a traditional Lutheran family, she was enraptured by dance at the tender age of 6. For a little girl living inside her head in Oshkosh, Wisconsin, dance represented freedom and a means to articulate gratitude, joy, and peace. It was also her solace during personal strife. "Music and dance make me feel alive and energized," she says. "I see life in art."

Like many young people, Magnuson wanted to parlay her passion into a career. This decision set her on what seemed to be an odd path: She traveled to Utah to attend Brigham Young University. At the time, Magnuson felt the choice was not only logical but also practical. BYU had an excellent and respected musical-theater program, and they offered her a scholarship.

The two years she spent at BYU were a period of rich self-discovery and painful self-doubt; of creative growth and repressed individuality. The Mormon juggernaut unleashed its infamous pressure to convert, and Magnuson felt politely yet persistently under siege during most of her tenure there. "My views and beliefs were under constant scrutiny," she states matter-of-factly. "I was questioned repeatedly about why I wasn't Mormon."

Most frustrating for Magnuson was an inability to dialogue comfortably about the loaded questions of religion, spirituality, and faith. She knew instinctively what her beliefs were; however, she lacked an in-depth biblical background and found herself mute to the increasing challenges of well-intentioned peers and counselors.

Refusing to give in to the colossus, Magnuson instead began exploring her spiritual side. She was determined to grow in her faith and was inspired to study the Bible and the teachings of Christ. "I found and joined a really good Christian group, and it gave me a foundation to find a more personal relationship with Christ, " she explains.

During this time, Magnuson experienced a personal epiphany of sorts: She decided she no longer wanted a career in dance. She did not lose her joy in or desire to dance; instead, she gradually realized that what we do for creative expression often becomes, well, *work*, when we use it to put food on the table. This revelation coincided with her decision to leave BYU. "I really felt that God was drawing me to something else," Magnuson says, "Not to leave or abandon my passion but to incorporate it and use it in a different way."

After transferring to Oral Roberts University, Magnuson began studying theology. "I didn't quite know where I was going with it, but I trusted God – which is hard sometimes!" She stumbled upon the marriage and family counseling program completely by accident, yet soon realized she had found her calling. Remembering her own parents' divorce, Magnuson states that it was the guidance and prayers of a loving network of friends and mentors that helped her through this turbulent period. "I had an incredible group of people who supported me through that difficult time – teachers, dance coaches, and youth group leaders, and I realized I wanted to do the same for others. It's another one of my passions. I so believe in marriage and strong families with a foundation in the church."

Dance, however, remains a vital part of Magnuson's life. A part-time dance instructor, she also is part of a touring company that uses dance to teach multiculturalism to elementary students – a tangible testament to dance's power to communicate across the gaps of cultural divides. "Art 'speaks' to people and reaches them in ways nothing else can," she says.

Her background in the arts and her entrance into the practice of family counseling give Magnuson rare insight on creativity, spirituality, and their connection to emotional healing. She hopes to use this unique perspective when counseling clients.

"Someone who is suffering emotionally or spiritually can definitely be helped by finding a creative outlet," says Magnuson, who adds that the process of expressing emotions like pain, grief, loss, and anger through creative means brings a sense of freedom, joy – and release. Examples abound as to the beneficial effects of both creating and viewing art. Movement and dance therapy have been successful in treating Post-Traumatic Stress Disorder, whose sufferers have been rendered silent by the turbulence in their lives. The success of the AIDS Quilt project also demonstrated profoundly the healing and uniting effects of art.

Magnuson believes that with art, we are emulating the ultimate Creator and, therefore, forging a connection to him. For many people, building this connection - or repairing a damaged one - is the first step toward healing their psyches and their souls. "God speaks to us through painting, poems, music, lyrics, dance, movement. And when we create, we are speaking back," she says.

Magnuson's definition of art extends far beyond the traditional one. "Some individuals claim that they are not 'creative types,' yet God still uses them through creative means," she says. According to Magnuson, anything can be an act of creation: Cooking. Repairing an engine. Gardening. The ability to love. "When we use our gifts – whatever they may be – we are glorifying God," she says.

We can turn to the potter's wheel, or the workbench, the barre, or the canvas when misery or strife render us silent. Our bodies, our hands, our eyes are as capable of speech as our mouths. Dance and art are languages of the soul, a kinetic form of prayer that can bring us closer to God – and each other.

ജ‍‍ൽ

Questions:

1. The pressure to conform can be powerful. Has God helped you resist this pressure? How?
2. Have your Christian beliefs ever come under fire? How did you react?
3. Discuss a time when your trust in God was rewarded.
4. We are all blessed with unique and special gifts. What are yours?
5. How can tapping into your creative natures bring us closer to God?

Dr. Jennifer Daniell

Jennifer Daniell graduated from Butler University in Indianapolis, Indiana in 1982 with a B.S. degree in psychology. In 1991 she earned her Ph.D. in psychology from Oklahoma State University, Stillwater, Oklahoma. From 1987 – 2000 she worked as a full time psychologist at Children's Medical Center (CMC), Tulsa, Oklahoma. Between 2000 and 2003 she worked part time for CMC in their outreach clinic and worked part time to establish her private practice, which she entered full time in 2003. Her practice consists of children, as young as the age of 2, as well as all ages through adulthood. She is a member of the American Psychological Association (APA.) Her church membership is at Fellowship Lutheran Church, Tulsa, Oklahoma.

From Indianapolis, Indiana, Daniell is the daughter of a zoology professor. No wonder her interests include gardening, watching dolphins and shore birds, collecting shells and beach walking along the ocean, especially on the beach of Port Aransas, Texas. She also spends time visiting family, which, in addition to her parents and brother in Indianapolis, also includes her sister, brother-in-law, and her toddler niece, Mae, in Baton Rouge, Louisiana.

God, Angels, and the Devil

ഇൗ

*People were bringing little children to him in order that he might
touch them; and the disciples spoke sternly to them. But when
Jesus saw this, he was indignant and said to them, "Let the little
children come to me, do not stop them; for it is to such as these
that the kingdom of God belongs. Truly, I tell you, whoever does
not receive the kingdom of God as a little child will never enter
it." And he took them up in his arms, laid his hands on them,
and blessed them.   (Mark 10: 13-16)*

Jennifer Daniell recalls the story of one
young boy who suffered from frightening
nightmares. He had awakened his parents so
often that they were not getting the sleep they needed.
The parents told this child he would have to handle the
nightmares by himself, so he had devised his own routine
when he awakened from a scary dream. He would pull
the covers up over his head, and then very quietly talk
to God, because God was always awake, and unlike his
parents, God didn't mind conversations in the middle of
the night.

Daniell finds when she works with children, especially those who have been traumatized, she often feels the presence of God. "These children often talk about God," Daniell said, "without being asked. Their spiritual, emotional and mental processes interact. For them, spirituality is simple, and they talk about it in terms of good and evil, God and angels and the devil." She describes how children try to take control of the bad encounters in their lives by "counteracting the evil source with a connection to the good source."

Daniell finds that most of the children who come to her for help have major behavioral problems as a result of parental abuse, neglect, or lack of proper treatment. Some of her young clients are genetically or developmentally disabled, and come seeking help in coping with these disabilities. Daniell often asks herself, "Why did bad things happen to these innocent children?" She says she has no answer to the question, except that working with them gives her strength as she observes the resilience and strength of the children.

Her caring response to children in need may be the result of her own childhood experience. When Daniell was seventeen, doctors found a growth in her brain. She remembers how she relied on her faith to get her through the uncertain times, the surgery and the recovery. Her faith "solidified," and has been a continuing source of strength for her. Her family calls it "blind faith." To Daniell there is nothing "blind" about it.

When she was growing up in her native Indiana, Daniell felt different from most of her friends and neighbors because she went to church. She stated that now, living in Tulsa, Oklahoma, "church-going" is more common. The people in her childhood Lutheran church taught her, "We are all connected," an understanding that she still believes and uses in her practice, as well as in her everyday life. That understanding of connectedness also led her to value acceptance and openness, other values which she uses in her therapy with children.

Daniell also learned the concept of "hope" from her Christian/Lutheran background. It too may have solidified when she was seventeen and relied on hope as well as her faith to get her through. It has endured because she exercises hope every day with her young clients. Daniell states, "The concept of hope is directly related to spirituality, and it is a really important thing for therapists to feel." Clients perceive hope, or the absence of hope, in a therapist's attitude and approach to their problem.

Her church, and the teachings she learned there, are also the reason why Daniell says she would never be involved in any kind of professional "ethical trap." She is not the type to "bend rules," and finds it hard to believe that any professional would.

> *"The concept of hope is directly related to spirituality, and it is a really important thing for therapists to feel."*

She acknowledges there are certain kinds of therapy that do not fit in with her spirituality, such as some aversive behavior modification techniques and strong confrontational styles.

When asked about her training, Daniell replied she was taught to keep herself "out of the therapeutic process." But her experience has taught her it is not possible. Daniell also believes that to keep herself separate from the therapeutic process would be counter-productive. Although she is open to other's values, she cannot practice outside her own values and beliefs.

Parents quite often ask Daniell if she is a Christian before they will schedule an appointment for their child. If they ask, she will tell them. It is not something she advertises. She does not pray with her clients, but every once in a while a parent or child will tell her that he/she has been praying for her.

"Some religious organizations are very helpful to children," Daniell states. "I see a lot of kids who have a hard time being accepted in their daily life. Several of my clients have joined a Christian youth organization called AWANA. In it they are immediately accepted as part of the group." Daniell again emphasizes the importance of acceptance as a Christian value, and how it is of utmost importance to vulnerable children. She also finds it important to teens. She states that many teen-age church groups teach the value of abstinence, which is a message teenagers may not be hearing anywhere else.

Though in her practice Daniell works mostly with children, in her training Daniell met with an extraordinary adult who taught her about the importance of spiritual grounding. "I'd never had such an ill person before," she said. This woman, we'll call her Alice, "came into my office, sat on the couch, and climbed into the fetal position. She was very damaged." Daniell went on to explain that Alice had been physically and emotionally abused as a child. After trust was established between client and therapist, Alice related something to Daniell that she had never told another person. Alice thought she had seen her parents murder her younger sibling. Keeping that secret had been so emotionally damaging to her that in her 20's she had joined a religious cult. Instead of teaching forgiveness, the members of the cult "served to shame and blame her." As an adult Alice suffered from post traumatic stress disorder (PTSD) and a personality disorder. Since Alice also had some medical problems, she went to see her doctor. The doctor told Alice that what she really needed was a healthy church experience. He recommended she attend his church, which she did. Over time this healthy church experience "transformed her, both physically and emotionally." She attributed her positive change to a "powerful, spiritual connection."

Daniell was curious, and asked Alice if the transformation she felt was from the support of the people in the congregation. Alice told her, "no," she really had not made any social connections at the church. What made the difference? Alice said, "The worship experience and the choir music." Daniell believes that when Alice's "internal beliefs kicked in," she began to heal.

Psychologists know when people have been traumatized or suffer from a psychotic disorder, God and devil images often come out in his/her delusions. This begs the question: "Is our spirituality hard-wired into our brain?" No matter where this phenomenon comes from, Daniell believes it helps the injured person "feel better."

Daniell learned a valuable lesson from her teenage life and death experience. And she continues to learn from her young clients. Whether it is called "blind faith," or "God, angels and the devil," a religious delusion, or talking to God under the covers at night, the desire for "a powerful spiritual connection," seems universal. Daniell is convinced that when that connection is made, our "spiritual, emotional and mental processes" come together and healing is possible.

಄಄

Questions:

1. What does it mean "to receive the kingdom of God as a little child?" What doesn't it mean?
2. How did you relate to God when you were a child, a teenager, a young adult, an older adult? How has it changed? What have you gained? What have you lost?
3. Was there a time when you relied solely on faith to get you through a terrible experience? Did it strengthen or weaken your faith? What is "blind faith?" What would "seeing faith" be like?
4. Daniell expresses the values of connectedness, acceptance, and openness in her life and practice. How do those values fit into your life and your interactions with people of other cultures, religions, age or sex?
5. Think about your own church experience. Is it healthy? Are there unhealthy aspects of your church environment? Are you able to openly discuss and resolve differences? Does one person (or a small group of persons) always make the decisions?

Gail Flack

Gail Flack attended Buena Vista University in Storm Lake, Iowa, where she received her B.A. in 1996. After obtaining her degree, Flack worked at a long-term care facility in Elk Horn, Iowa for four years with the aging population, where she says her sense of spirituality and growth of understanding about the power of "presence as prayer" was developed.

The wife of an ELCA Pastor, Flack moved to Tulsa, Oklahoma, where her husband was called to serve in 2001. She managed and supervised the staff of LIFE Senior Services Adult Day Service Programs until 2003 and is currently on staff at Laureate Psychiatric Hospital in Tulsa. Flack is enrolled in a graduate program of social work at the University of Oklahoma and will soon become a member of the National Association of Social Workers.

Her interests include music, reading, camping, hiking, and enjoying time with family. Flack has written sacred music and continues to seek creative expression through music. Other deep interests include social justice issues, particularly the alleviation of poverty and homelessness and the civil rights of minority groups, such as gay and lesbian groups, as well as Asian, Hispanic, and African-American citizens.

Flack and her husband, Sidney, belong to the Lutheran Church of the Prince of Peace in Tulsa. The couple has two grown children, John and Miriam.

Presence as Prayer

∞

"For I am convinced that neither death, nor life, nor angels, nor rulers, nor things present, nor things to come, nor powers, nor height, nor depth, nor anything else in all creation, will be able to separate us from the love of God in Christ Jesus our Lord."
(Romans 8: 38-39)

An elderly nursing home resident is near death. She suffers from Alzheimer's disease and is barely aware of her surroundings, unaware that the room she has been moved to is a hospice room. Her son and daughter-in-law come to visit and bring with them other family members who love the dying woman.

When the whole family is gathered, they begin to rub the woman's feet. They hold her hand, cry, and stroke her. They run fingers through her hair. While they are doing this, they speak words of life to her. They tell her about the good life she has led and about the fine son she has raised. "You've given us all so much and we love you," they tell her, "but God loves you too, and God wants you now." The woman dies peacefully, at rest in the conviction of her family's final benediction.

"It was the most powerful thing I've experienced," says Gail Flack of this incident she witnessed when she worked at a nursing home in Iowa. "Although this woman probably wasn't cognizant of the words that were said in the hours just prior to her death, it was clear that being surrounded by her family and being physically loved by them—through their touching her—invoked God's presence for her and for the whole family." As a social worker who is committed to working with older persons, Flack says she's witnessed similar situations many times as she sat with families while their loved ones were dying.

Caring for older persons requires patience and understanding. When those persons are also affected by dementia or Alzheimer's disease, there are additional challenges for caregivers. According to Flack, "a person with dementia doesn't respond in the same way as another older person might. You have to pray differently with them." There might be less awareness of what is happening around them, but Flack says there is still awareness of God. "Their spirituality is not concrete, but is experienced as a perceived awareness of God's presence."

Flack worked for several years in the Iowa nursing home and then in an adult day care center in Tulsa. "Sometimes what I thought was most helpful was to remain calm and just let people know I was there." With such people, Flack says, "prayer becomes simply touching, holding hands, being with them and letting them know you're there. Prayer is more tactile for them."

Flack remembers another patient at the nursing home. "His name was Sidney, the same as my husband. I used to call him my 'other Sidney.' One Christmas he invited me to listen to a compact disc he had. It was a recording of Christmas music sung by Charlotte Church. He wanted me to listen with him to 'Ave Maria.' As we listened, he held my hand and tears rolled down his face. It was hard for me not to cry with him. When it was over, he said, 'that's the most beautiful song I've ever heard.' It was a spiritual moment and solidified an emotional relationship between us." Flack says after that night, she often spent time with Sidney, holding his hand and talking with him about their shared love of classical music and other things, through the time before his death when he was not very responsive to her presence. "The act of sitting with him and talking to him, while he understood I was there to take care of him, was a spiritual one," she says.

"Prayer becomes simply touching, holding hands, being with them and letting them know you're there. Prayer is more tactile for them."

Among both the nursing home patients and day care participants, activities that focus on increasing cognitive awareness are stressed to delay an inevitable decline of abilities. "Although their cognitive abilities decline," Flack says, "there's still an opportunity to work with them." Some older persons with severe dementia are unable to benefit from such activities, however. Flack believes her Christian perspective helps her approach those persons with compassion. "I have an understanding that God works through them, in spite of their limited capacity to understand."

When Flack's husband Sidney was called to serve as the pastor of a church in Tulsa a few years ago, Flack says she experienced a sort of culture shock. She had been working in a Danish community in Iowa, where she says most of the residents of the nursing home were stoics. "They don't say some things out loud. They're reserved." One woman had been raised a Roman Catholic and was worried about being in a Lutheran nursing home. "I had to laugh. I tried to reassure her that God loved her whether she was in a Catholic nursing home or a Lutheran home."

From this environment, Flack was suddenly transplanted to the Oklahoma Bible Belt. "Many of the people I work with, most of whom consider themselves Christian, believe God has given them their afflictions. They think, 'This is the way God wants me to be, because God has planned everything.' There is a prayer for every event that happens in their lives. They also say 'I've chosen to walk this life', or that 'I've chosen to follow Christ and obtain spirituality.'" Flacks says that contrasts with her personal belief that, "God chooses us."

While her move to Oklahoma meant adjusting to different attitudes toward spirituality, "It wasn't difficult. In fact, it's been a breath of fresh air. The day care participants are not inhibited in their expression. It is really interesting. You always know where they're coming from." She has felt herself becoming more open to the variety of faith expressions she has experienced in Oklahoma. "At first I was amused by the differences, but their faith is sincere," she says, and that makes it possible to find genuine areas of agreement.

Flack says that most of the staff at the adult day care center are professing Christians, though some of the supervisors are not. Staff generally feel free to discuss spiritual issues with center participants who wish to and even to pray with them on occasion. "I pray every day *for* the staff and the center participants, too," Flack says. "They may not hear it, but I say it. It's important for the demented to know they're loved, particularly when they come from chaotic households where they do strange things that cause stress on the family." Another way in which her faith informs her work is in a deeply felt principle: "I won't be the judge of others," she says. "For many of these people, too many have already judged them and they don't need me judging them, too."

Because of the amount of time she spends with elderly persons, Flack says that end-of-life issues inevitably arise in her work. "End-of-life issues were encountered often with the families of our patients in the nursing home.

We had many spiritual conversations when the patient was not aware of what was being discussed. Family members, though, needed the comfort of knowing that God had blessed their loved one through a compassionate person who was taking care of them.

"It's interesting that people don't always invoke the name of Christian as who they are. At the end of life, people tend to go back, tend to seek God's presence. Even if they haven't been going to church and even if they don't admit it, what they long for is God's presence. It's a time for family members to remember the loved one and the history they've shared. They want to be able to tell their loved one that 'God will take care of you'. Emotions are high and powerful; they want to be a part of this person they love and so they do this by going back to what their parent or loved one believed in the past. For many, this past includes Christian beliefs or participation in a church."

It's no coincidence that Flack recognizes so clearly the ministry of presence in her daily work. "I did clinical pastoral education in Cherokee, Iowa at a mental health institute with a wise priest who gave me a sense of spirituality and helped me understand the presence of God in almost every situation."

During her training, Flack worked with a young boy who had multiple problems, including Attention Deficit Hyperactivity Disorder. "He was a kid in trouble; he would get kicked off the bus or fail to do his work, and then he'd get sent to the principal—sometimes three or four times a week." Flack says she often went to the principal's office with him, and she often took the principal's side. In spite of that, she always expressed faith in the boy. "I kept asking him to tell us what he needed to succeed. I always thanked him for doing a good job when he did his work. Eventually, he got to the point where he could stay on the bus, stay in class, and stay out of the principal's office." She saw the boy once a week, and thinks that what was most valuable about their meetings was simply being there with him. "I was a trustworthy presence in his life," Flack says, something she felt he had been missing, but that was very important. "He knew I enjoyed being with him, and that made all the difference in the world. I think this is an example of spiritual healing, even if the boy didn't really have a concept of God."

In addition to her exposure to a Christian mentor, Flack is both the wife of a Lutheran pastor and the daughter of a Lutheran pastor—a tenth generation Lutheran pastor. It's a heritage that can be overwhelming at times, she says. It also contributes to unrealistic expectations from others about her. "The people I work with are curious about me when they learn I'm a Lutheran pastor's wife and they respond differently to me because of it." It's a role that's sometimes difficult for Flack to fill and one that's been ever present in her life. "As the pastor's wife, you have to be part of the congregation, yet not really a part of it."

> *Flack has learned to be open to her patients' needs . . . prayer might mean simply "being with them while they're hallucinating or having delusions."*

Mythical expectations of what Christianity is can sometimes be trouble for others as well. Religious practices are not always fond memories for family members of the people she serves. "Some have turned away because of a parent's domineering nature or demands that their children attend church." In cases of mental illness, patients are not always able to differentiate between God and the visual or auditory hallucinations that are hallmarks of their illness. "Some patients with schizophrenia attribute good voices to that of God, and bad voices to the devil." Flack has learned to be open to her patients' needs and says in those cases, prayer might mean simply "being with them while they're hallucinating or having delusions."

Among the elderly, she offers a different sort of

presence. "The elderly have learned to deal with conflict and disappointment. They learn acceptance, which makes end-of-life issues somewhat easier for them." Flack says some never learn to accept death, but in general, she thinks most older people are not afraid of death.

"End-of-life issues may be understood differently by those who are Christian," she says. "They understand that God is in control of their lives and see death as an opportunity to meet their God face to face."

Flack says there are also those elderly who have only found God at the end of their lives, and although they find comfort in that, they may not experience the depth of understanding as one who has grown in faith throughout life. "They don't understand the power of God or the subtleties of God."

Flack recognizes that when her presence aids in a person's healing, it isn't she alone who effects healing, but the Holy Spirit within her. There are, in turn, those who embody the spirit through small acts of love that build her up for her work. "These acts demonstrate the subtleties of God, I think."

Her profound awareness of how faith affects her work and the emotional health of those in her care—no matter where they see God in their lives—leaves her open to new career challenges. "I'm open to where the journey will take me," Flack says. Wherever she feels called to serve along the way, she will bring the same spiritual values of presence and touch to her work. For Flack, the Holy Spirit is as tangible and physical as the touch of one hand on another.

☙❧

Questions:

1. What comfort does this scripture passage from Romans (8:38-39) provide about our inseparability from God's love? Why might it provide greater comfort to those near death?
2. Have you spent time with someone very ill or near their death? If so, have you experienced a sense, like Flack's, that your presence is all that is required of you.
3. How do we sometimes fail to provide comfort to those in pain or near death by thinking we must do or say something?
4. How can older persons who have a deep confidence in death as an "opportunity to meet God," help younger, or other older persons grow in trusting God?

Dr. Ondria Gleason

Ondria Gleason received her Bachelor of Arts degree from Hastings College in Hastings, Nebraska, and her M.D. from the University of Nebraska Medical Center in Omaha, Nebraska. She has served in various faculty positions for the University of Oklahoma College of Medicine, including Vice Chairman of the Department of Psychiatry and Director of Psychiatry Residency Training. She has provided psychiatric services at Hillcrest Medical Center and Laureate Psychiatric Clinic and Hospital in Tulsa, Oklahoma. She is certified by the American Board of Psychiatry and Neurology and holds medical licenses in both Oklahoma and Iowa. She is a member of the American Psychiatric Association, Academy of Psychosomatic Medicine, Oklahoma Psychiatric Physicians' Association, and the Association of Director's of Medical Student Education in Psychiatry.

Gleason has published over 20 articles and medical abstracts in publications such as *Psychosomatics, Medicine and Psychiatry, American Family Physician*, and the *Journal of Clinical Psychiatry*, and has been a Principal Investigator in three pharmacological research projects. She frequently presents lectures and seminars to medical students, and psychiatry residents, and as a guest lecturer to other medical and teaching institutions.

Gleason and her husband Scott have two children, Bradley and Zachary. She attends Fellowship Lutheran Church where she has been a Sunday School teacher and serves on the Mental Health Advisory Committee for outreach to Guyana. In 2001, she participated in the Partners in Mission trip to Guyana, South America.

Lighting the Lamp

₰Ↄଓ

"No one after lighting a lamp puts it in a cellar, but on the
lampstand so that those who enter may see the light. Your eye is
the lamp of your body. If your eye is healthy, your whole body is
full of light; but if it is not healthy, your body is full of darkness.
Therefore consider whether the light in you is not darkness.
If then your whole body is full of light, with no part of it in
darkness, it will be as full of light as when a lamp gives you light
with its rays." (Luke 11: 33-36)

"I can't believe he told you he's Baptist. Dr.
Gleason, my father always told us kids
that there's no such thing as God or life
after death," she said, continuing to look at her father's
psychiatrist in disbelief. Dr. Gleason nodded at her
patient's daughter, recalling his painful expression when
they discussed his diagnosis of terminal cancer.

"You go to dust! That's what he always said. You
just go to dust when you die." She was still coping with
her father's illness and his change of heart.

"He's willing to open the door to his faith, no
matter how long it has been shut. He needs that now,"
replied Dr. Gleason, not surprised at the abrupt change in

her patient's beliefs. She knew her patient was willing to open the door to his faith in his time of need, however long that door had been closed. And he was willing to do so, even though his daughter believed he had shut that door completely.

Dr. Ondria Gleason acknowledges, even with her strong personal convictions, that sharing religious belief in a professional environment is more art than science. "We're taught not to share information about ourselves with patients and, even more, not to influence patients with our own religious beliefs," Gleason explains when asked about using her spiritual background in her professional practice. "But my beliefs as a Christian certainly make it easier for me to question patients about their own beliefs, potentially bringing out another means for them to cope with their problems. Asking someone if they have a religious background, for example, allows me to introduce the subject without implying that the patient is currently active in their faith. The patient can question themselves about whether or not this is an option for coping with their problems, and it can be a very helpful exercise."

"We're taught not to share information about ourselves with patients, and even more, not to influence patients with our own religious beliefs."

Gleason has a unique perspective on helping others in the field of mental health. Unlike many psychiatrists who work exclusively with patients, Gleason's devotion lies as much with helping and educating other professionals as it does with helping patients. She is not only a psychiatrist, but also a teacher and collaborator, providing clinical instruction to medical school students and psychiatric resident physicians, and consultative service to physicians of other specialties.

Gleason's confidence in her work and her beliefs is obvious, and it's easy to understand her success in teaching and advising others. She solidly explains her own connection to Christianity and her belief that faith can be a foundation for staying healthy in all aspects of life. It becomes even clearer as she speaks that, once she established that strong foundation for herself, she was committed to helping others do the same.

Gleason attended medical school with the intent of becoming a family medical doctor, but became seriously interested in psychiatry during medical school at the University of Nebraska. Like all medical students, she was required to complete a psychiatry clerkship, and she found that she enjoyed the type of interaction with people that this field requires. She also recognized quickly that by helping people mentally, you actually help them in a much broader way, including social and physical health. "It seemed like a way to do more of God's work," she says.

Gleason has seen a variety of ways in which Christian thinking can impact the doctor-patient relationships and the outcome of treatments. "In some ways, Christian beliefs provide very pragmatic preventive medicine. Patients considering suicide, for example, may unilaterally eliminate that option because the proposition of 'hell' looms before them. While it doesn't solve their problems, a patient's belief may require him to face his problems instead of giving up, and even ending his life." Gleason explains.

Gleason acknowledges that evangelism is an important part of being a Christian, but stresses that introducing Christianity in a physician-patient situation can be tricky. "It has to be handled carefully, and timing is very important," Gleason emphasizes. She adds, "The patient's needs always have to be the first priority." She recalls having some problems with residents who are "assertively" Christian. "While the intent may be good, it can be a problem if a rapport has not been established with the patient first." She remembers one case where the resident would pray with patients even if they had not asked him to. This resident's approach prompted letters of complaint when he persisted, regardless of negative feedback from patients. Ultimately, this resident went on to have a successful Christian psychiatry practice, where his patients selected him specifically because of his knowledge as a psychiatrist, and because he incorporated his beliefs as a Christian into his practice.

Conversely, Gleason says patients have asked her if she is a Christian and if she will pray with them. Because she is a Christian and is comfortable in such a situation, she finds that it can provide an immediate connection and rapport with the patient, allowing other healing work to progress more quickly.

"My belief in God gives purpose to what I do, and it helps me stay focused on what helps the patient. Very fundamentally, when life is stressful, you need a place to go for strength. Having that resource helps my marriage, my family, my work, and virtually all aspects of my life. And that allows me to help others."

Gleason describes a useful lesson from her college days, given by her sponsor in the Fellowship of Christian Athletes. At that time, she faced a myriad of issues and decisions from practically every aspect of her life. Her sponsor drew a diagram of how she seemed to be approaching her decision making process. The diagram had Gleason in the middle with all other aspects of her life, including Christ, surrounding her. He then drew a picture of an alternate way to view her life, one that puts Christ in the center instead of her.

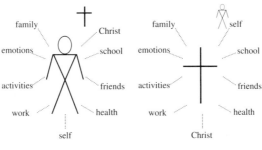

Self-centered life = chaos   *Christ-centered life = order*

74

This guidance gave her a new perspective on dealing with day-to-day issues. "If I clearly establish my values first and use those values to direct all aspects of my life, then I don't have to constantly evaluate decisions and second-guess myself." She uses this same concept today when teaching third and fourth year medical students, residents of all levels and even in working with other doctors in the hospital. In essence, keeping Christ at the center of her decision-making is an enlightening process and has even allowed her to share this enlightenment with her colleagues and students. "I see pain and confusion all the time. If I can show people how to maintain a simple, healthy life, established on Christian values, then many times the other problems can be avoided or dealt with more effectively."

Gleason believes being a Christian filters into everything she does. Those basic values she learned in her Christian education have carried over into her work life. *Put the interests of others before your own; follow through on commitments; always do your best.* These are all just basic beliefs, learned as a Christian and tied to biblical reference, but applied to daily living. The ability to apply our beliefs separates us from those who don't have a strong foundation of values to draw upon. "In decision making, it's easy to detect when a person chooses the path of least resistance or makes a decision to please someone else instead of standing by their values," she says.

Like light from a lamp, our beliefs filter into all aspects of our lives. Gleason sees this as a challenge to be tackled and an opportunity for every person who's willing to open themselves to a better decision-making process. And it's clear that when given the chance, she'll create a light in the lives of those she touches.

ℰ᎒℧Ꮪ

Questions:

1. Luke 11: 33-36 refers to our eyes as the lamp of our body. "If your eye is healthy, your body will be full of light." What can you do to keep your eye healthy and your body full of light? Do you have examples of times when keeping your eye healthy did bring light to other parts of your life?
2. How often do you put your lamp in the cellar? On the lampstand? What causes you to do one or the other?
3. What activities can you commit to in order to ensure that you keep your eye healthy and your lamp on the lampstand?
4. How does your Christian belief filter in to various aspects of your life? How does it filter into the lives of others?

Cynthia Gustavson

Cynthia Gustavson attended Gustavus Adolphus College, graduated from Boston University, and earned an M.S.W. from Louisiana State University. She did graduate work in theology at United Seminary of the Twin Cities, and doctoral work in education at Oklahoma State University. She is currently a psychotherapist at the Center for Counseling and Education, a pastoral counseling center in Tulsa, OK.

Cynthia is the author of two books, a poetry book, *Scents of Place: Seasons of the St. Croix Valley,* 1987 (Country Messenger Press, Marine on St. Croix, MN) and a book of poetry therapy, *In-Versing Your Life: A Poetry Workbook for Self-Discovery and Healing,* 1995 (Families Int., Inc. Milwaukee, WI.) She has been a guest lecturer at The Hilton Head Health Institute in SC. Her book, *Re-Versing the Numbers: A Poetry Workbook for Eating Disorders* is being considered for publication. Her poetry and articles about spirituality and poetry therapy have been printed in national magazines, including *The Christian Century, Sojourners, Lutheran Woman Today, The Journal of Poetry Therapy,* and *Families in Society.*

Cynthia, a native of Afton, Minnesota, now lives with her husband of 35 years, Dr. Ed Gustavson, in Tulsa, Oklahoma. They have two children, Britta, 32, and Kent, 25. She is currently on the advisory board of Trinity Ministries, a member of Tulsa Metro Ministries Legislative Committee, Tulsa Peace Fellowship, and a member of Fellowship Lutheran Church.

Permission Granted

*When I was a child, I spoke like a child, I thought like a child,
I reasoned like a child; when I became an adult, I put an end to
childish ways. For now we see in a mirror, dimly, but then we
will see face to face. Now I know only in part; then I will know
fully, even as I have been fully known. And now faith, hope and
love abide, these three; and the greatest of these is love.
(I Corinthians 13: 11-13)*

"When you see my mother," said a
perceptive 35-year-old man who
was about to bring his devout
Baptist mother in for counseling, "you will need to begin
each session with a prayer in which you ask for God's
counsel, and then at the end of each session you will
need to ask Mother to end with a prayer." This 65 year
old woman had been told by her family physician to seek
counseling because her high blood pressure and ulcers
were not responding to treatment. It was clear to her
family that this recent widow had something inside her
that needed to be addressed. Her children also knew that
their mother would never talk about an intimate issue with
anyone who was not a professing Christian.

"It was not my usual policy to pray with clients," said Cynthia Gustavson, "even though I'm a pastoral counselor. But since I'd had seminary training in addition to my social work degree, and had made it a policy to treat both mind and spirit, it was a request I could easily fulfill. For those who request it, an opening prayer serves not only to allow God into our discussions, but also to establish immediate trust between us."

In this case it was extremely important to establish trust, because on the day of the first session (unknown to Gustavson) this woman's son had driven her to Gustavson's office with no advance warning of where he was taking her. She had a hurt and puzzled look on her face as he brought her into the office, introduced her to the counselor, and then sat down and proceeded to tell her life story. After Gustavson had gently ousted him from her office, his mother and she had a rough start. The woman (we'll call her Audrey) told Gustavson that she didn't need counseling, and she couldn't believe her son had done this to her. Gustavson apologized to Audrey for the way this had been handled, and asked her if it would be all right to begin with a prayer. Audrey said, "Yes, please ask for Jesus' help."

Unbelievably, they talked. They connected. Audrey shared concerns she had never voiced before to anyone. At the end of that first session Audrey summed up her concerns in a prayer she offered to God. Audrey kept coming back, week after week, facing issues she had never been able to face before, each session beginning and ending with prayer. "It was important for her to know I was a Christian," said Gustavson, "and that I felt comfortable including God in the session, because her inner conflict included a spiritual crisis. She hadn't been able to talk to her pastor because he would not allow her to question God. And she had lots of questions about what she assumed were God's laws and actions."

After four months her ulcer was on the mend, she was able to incorporate forgiveness as a God-given gift, and she even began to look at scripture in a new light. During her last session with Gustavson, Audrey announced that she had stood up to her entire adult Sunday School class in her interpretation of the Old Testament story of David and Bathsheba. Audrey told the class that God not only forgave David once, when he sent Bathsheba's husband to battle and to his death, but God continued to forgive David every day of his life thereafter, even though David continued to live in sin by marrying and living with Bathsheba. She said, "Even when we know we are wrong, and we won't or can't change our ways, God still loves and forgives us. If he could continually forgive David, he can forgive me."

Most of the time prayer works in ways that are more subtle. There are times when a client's life problems seem so complex that Gustavson whispers a prayer to herself, "I need help with this one, God."

Most of the time prayer works in ways that are more subtle. There are times when a client's life problems seem so complex that Gustavson whispers a prayer to herself, "I need help with this one, God." She says that it never fails to clear her mind and help her concentrate on the healing path the session will take. She states, "I also feel the presence of God as I listen to the life stories of my clients. Each is so unique, and most are filled with pain. So many of their stories tell of lives that should have collapsed under the weight of adversity, but which were somehow sustained long enough to seek help and ensure healing."

Gustavson sees a large part of what she does as a granting of permission to let the human spirit and the Holy Spirit work their wonders. It is a gentle granting of permission to speak, to feel, to love, to listen, to forgive, to grieve, and then to end grieving, which opens blocked pathways and allows the free flow of healing.

One example Gustavson gave of permission-giving was of a woman we will call Helen. She came to Gustavson's office on January 13th. Helen was about to lose her job because on the 13th of every month she would fall apart emotionally. She couldn't concentrate, was tearful, was full of fatigue and a feeling of dread. She routinely called in sick on that day, and she was warned by her supervisor that she now had no more sick days available to her. When asked how long this had been going on she said "for 38 years."

Gustavson asked, "What happened 38 years ago on the 13th of a month?"

She said, "My mother died in a car accident." She was silent while she wiped the tears from her eyes, and then she finished, "and I was driving the car."

"You were just a teenager then?" Gustavson asked.

Helen replied, "Yes, I had just gotten my license."

Over the next several sessions they talked about what it was like to be a teenager, to learn something new. They talked about her mother and what her mother would want of her. They talked about God and her understanding of confession and forgiveness. And little by little Helen was reminded that she had permission to forgive herself and get on with her life.

Another time Gustavson felt that it was the simple act of giving permission which allowed healing was with a woman we will call Clara. She was a 72 year old woman who had immigrated to the U.S. from Germany with her husband after World War II. She had been raised in a strict German family, as had her husband. She now found herself alone. Her husband had died three years earlier, and her only daughter had been virtually disowned for decades because she lived by a different code than the strict and rigid value system of her parents. Clara hardly knew her teenage grandchildren even though they lived less than a mile away from her. After months in Gustavson's grief support group, one day Clara surprised the group by saying, "I'm over it."

"Over what?" replied the other members.

"Over him. It's been three years and now I'm over him."

Gustavson asked, "What does that mean?"

"Well," she said, "I called my daughter, and we're talking now." The group cheered. "And I've decided to live again."

It was amazing the transformation that everyone in the group saw. Clara's eyes sparkled. Her mouth was relaxed and formed a smile they had never seen before. Even her speech was more assertive and lively. The compassion of the grief support group members had given Clara permission to re-evaluate her life, to stop her grieving, and to love again.

Gustavson's favorite example of permission-giving is about a 15 year old girl we will call LaKesha. She had unwillingly come to one of Gustavson's support groups for new teen mothers. LaKesha came to the group, but never participated. She sat with her head down on the table and pretended to sleep. One day Gustavson asked the young girls to write a metaphor for their lives. They were to write: I used to be (fill in an object from nature) but now I am (another object from nature.) All of the members loved doing this exercise, and Gustavson noticed that even LaKesha had written something on her paper.

When it came time for LaKesha to read hers, she barely raised her head and whispered, "I used to be a beautiful flower, but now I am a stem, because I am broken." There was silence in the room, and then all of the girls started telling LaKesha that she was a poet, and how beautiful it was, and wasn't she proud. LaKesha sat upright, opened her eyes wide, and beamed. "Can I take my poem home to Mother?" she asked.

Gustavson took her aside before she left for home and said, "LaKesha, you have a gift. I want you to go home and think about your future, and write: I am a broken stem, but I will be …" Gustavson gave LaKesha permission to grieve and also to focus on a time when her grief would end.

Gustavson often uses poetry in her therapy. "I find poetry is the language of the spirit. Feelings which are deeply hidden or unexplainable can sometimes come to life in a metaphor or in the words of a poem."

Several years ago a mother from rural Grove, Oklahoma brought her 8 year old son to see Gustavson. The teacher had told this mother to bring Charlie to a counselor because he had been refusing to talk. It was okay at home if he wanted to be silent, but it didn't work at school. Both of his grandparents had died in the previous four months, and he had been present at their deaths. Both Charlie's Mom and Dad worked two jobs and he had grown up spending most of his time with these two grandparents who now were suddenly gone. Charlie was hurt not only by the trauma of seeing death first hand twice, but also by their absence in his life. The third wounding came because no one would talk about it. He was a boy, and he was supposed to go on as if nothing had happened. Gustavson read Shel Silverstein poems to Charlie. They played games, drew pictures of his beloved grandparents, used finger puppets to talk to them, and finally talked outright to one another about the loss and the love. Gustavson gave Charlie the permission his parents had denied him, to own his own feelings, and to find his own voice. When Charlie decided to speak, his voice was truly a gift of God.

Gustavson says there are hundreds of other stories about the giving of permission that allow the human spirit and the Holy Spirit to work toward healing. It happens in marriage counseling when partners give one another permission to listen to one another instead of defending themselves. It happens when she tells young women with low self-esteem that Jesus' words "love thy neighbor as thyself" means to love yourself first, and then love others the same way.

That same spirit allows Gustavson to permit herself

to be inspired by her own clients. She tells the story of one teenager whose father had been married three times, her mother (an alcoholic) four times. She had 14 step-sisters and brothers ranging in age from 34 down to 15. Her only full sister was mentally ill. Her only full brother was a high school dropout and drug addict. But this amazing girl was perfectly normal. She came weekly to talk to Gustavson, who became her touchstone to reality. Although she had a close relationship with her dad, she had no one to talk to about female things. She was open about the fact that her love of Jesus kept her normal, and that people at church were her mentors. The words of Jesus were her support. Through all the inappropriate phone calls and cries of help from her dysfunctional family, this young woman stood firm in her beliefs and goals. And although at times she felt as though she was a failure, because she could not change the behavior of those closest to her in her family, she inspired fellow students, fellow church members, extended family members and countless others who witnessed her life in Christ. "She came to me for help," says Gustavson, "but after an hour with her I always felt stronger, happier, and inspired."

"Psychology and theology may use different terminology," Gustavson states, "but they both try to describe the same processes that we all see and understand 'in a mirror, dimly'." In graduate school Gustavson was taught never to talk about anything in the therapy session that had to do with theological beliefs. In her national examinations spirituality was never even hinted at. But in trying to embrace wholeness, she realized that humans cannot be divided into separate parts that are treated differently. Body, mind, emotions and spirit are intertwined. She's glad that her clients never let her forget it. And she's glad that she feels God's permission to use her talent of poetry as well as other gifts to encourage the healing of others.

Questions:

1. Discuss the verse, *"for now we see in a mirror dimly,"* in terms of absolute knowledge of right and wrong, and in terms of the many interpretations of scripture reflected in the denominations of Christianity.

2. How has the verse, *"and the greatest of these is love,"* informed your Christian life?

3. Have you ever been angry with God? Have you ever questioned God's motives? Are you able to talk about your feelings about God with anyone? Is questioning God the "unforgivable sin?" Whom do you go to when even God seems to have abandoned you? Can you pray to God when you are angry with God?

4. Try the metaphor technique used in this chapter. Write: I used to be…(fill in an object from nature,) but now I am … (another object from nature.) Give yourself permission to say, I am … (nature object) but I will be … (a different nature object.) How does faith in God enable you to change?

5. Were there times in your life when you lost your voice, not physically, but spiritually or emotionally? What happened? How did you regain it? Did someone else give you permission to speak again? How does God give us permission?

Suzanne Davidson

Suzanne Davidson is currently a genetics counselor and regional medical specialist for Myriad Genetic Laboratories, where she provides medical education to health care professionals and the community about hereditary cancer. She is a member of the National Society of Genetic Counselors & Special Interest Groups, the American Board of Genetic Counselors, Oklahoma Genetics Advisory Council, and the Genetics Education Committee of Oklahoma.

Davidson was employed between 1999 and 2002 at the H.A. Chapman Institute of Medical Genetics in Tulsa, where she performed patient evaluation and genetic counseling with pediatric and adult patients. Much of her work there involved prenatal genetic counseling.

In 1996, Davidson received a B.S. in psychology from The University of Tulsa and an M.S. in Genetic Counseling from the University of Colorado Health Sciences Center in 1999. Her abstract and poster "Genetics in Primary Care: An Educational Initiative" was presented at the Genetics Counselors Annual Education Conference in 2001.

Hobbies and interests include University of Tulsa basketball, volleyball, dancing, reading, writing, snow and water skiing, and playing the clarinet. Davidson is active in church music ministry programs and serves as a congregational leader. She and husband Danny were members of Fellowship Lutheran Church in Tulsa, but now live in Colorado.

The Fragrance of Christ

ဆၣ

But thanks be to God, who in Christ always leads us in triumphal procession, and through us spreads in every place the fragrance that comes from knowing him. For we are the aroma of Christ to God among those who are being saved and among those who are perishing; to the one a fragrance from death to death, to the other a fragrance from life to life. Who is sufficient for these things? For we are not peddlers of God's word like so many; but in Christ we speak as persons of sincerity, as persons sent from God and standing in his presence. (2 Corin. 2: 14-17)

Can I cope with a child that has genetic abnormalities? Should I abort this pregnancy? Will this abnormality mean an early death? Why would God create a human being who is doomed to suffer?

These are questions most of us never need to ask. For those who find themselves faced with the need to ask them, however, the answers are rarely clear or painless. When it's discovered that a child or fetus has inherited genetic abnormalities that will result in suffering and perhaps early death, parents have agonizing choices to make. On the other hand, adult patients who learn that their genes are inherently abnormal and will likely lead to cancer or other diseases are faced with few choices. A genetics counselor like Suzanne Davidson can provide invaluable support as patients move toward understanding and acceptance of genetic defects.

"My role is one of giving information and listening," Davidson says. As such, it is important to maintain a level of impartiality. "It isn't appropriate to express my personal views about faith to patients. I am neutral and non-directive. In our training, we were taught awareness of other cultures and religious practices; spiritual awareness. It was expected that our own beliefs would play a role in how we reacted as counselors," she says, "but should not be expressed."

"There was more emphasis placed on the awareness of spirituality issues during graduate school, but it was ingrained in us to be neutral and non-directive in dealing with patients. There are statements in our ethics guidelines and our professional statement which indicate that influencing patients with our own beliefs is inappropriate." In spite of this, Davidson is well aware that personal spirituality plays an important role in how couples handle decision making. She says she draws heavily on her own faith in God to provide encouragement to her patients.

Without drawing her faith into discussions with patients then, Davidson is able to invite the Holy Spirit into their interactions through her own prayers. Bringing the Holy Spirit into her counseling sessions gives comfort to Davidson and, by extension, to her patients. The apostle Paul, in his second letter to the Corinthians, would recognize this as spreading "in every place the fragrance that comes from knowing him (Christ)." It's an unusual but evocative image.

A genetics counselor sees children with birth defects, patients with a family history of cancer or neurological disorders, as well as pregnant women faced with risk factors or decisions to continue or terminate a pregnancy. Some patients with family histories of genetic abnormalities come to Davidson to make decisions about whether or not to test for familial problems. About half of her patients are children; about half are adults. Choosing to test for a genetic defect at all is sometimes as agonizing as dealing with the test results themselves, particularly in cases where effective treatments aren't available. Sometimes the only choice is to simply accept the results.

Davidson witnesses many reactions to the painful news of test results. "Countless patients, when faced with difficult circumstances, when they learn their baby has a genetic disorder, contend that the circumstance must be God's will, or that the outcome is up to God. Some ask, 'Why is this happening to me?' and others simply say, 'It's in God's hands.'" Though her patients are often eager to express their faith in such statements, Davidson says she is never asked to pray with them. "I was once asked to go to a Bible study with a patient, though," she says, an offer she declined. Davidson says she often prays for patients without their knowing it. "I sometimes pray for a client with a particular issue to deal with, whether or not it's something they are doing on their own. It's something I do if I feel close to a patient, or if I know they're going through a difficult time, but it's not something I bring up with them," she says.

"Typically, patients don't know I'm Christian," Davidson continues. She thinks her reaction to their statements about their faith might sometimes convey that fact, even when she does not state it. "My reaction depends on the situation and what they're dealing with. It's comforting to know that God is present, even when they do not. I usually mirror their statements. When they say, 'I know God is with my child,' I mirror that."

As a Christian, Davidson feels she faces a bit more difficulty than her non-Christian professional colleagues, because it's sometimes hard to hear her patients' ideas about where God is (or isn't) in their particular situation. Yet, she's there to provide information and encouragement, and she does so without comment on their beliefs. "It isn't an issue with some of my colleagues in the science fields," she said. "Faith isn't an integral part of their lives."

Davidson's faith provides both challenges and blessings for her in her work, however. "My own ability to do this work day in and day out is dependent on my faith. I derive more internal and personal rewards than others might. It's comforting to know that God is there for the patient. And it means a lot for me personally. There are a lot of good outcomes and a lot of bad outcomes as well," she says.

"Many times, when patients are open about their faith, they are more at peace over their situation and their decision. It's definitely a help." She cites cases of pregnant women who are faced with a choice to continue or terminate a pregnancy as an example. "For some, their faith guides them. And even when God's presence isn't mentioned, I feel it in abstract ways, in terms of confidence going in or when I am having a difficult time with a patient. It's more of a comfort to me in preparing to see a patient when I'm giving them bad news if I know I'm not going in alone."

While Davidson is careful not to influence her patients by directing conversations to personal faith, her experiences as a genetic counselor have influenced her own faith. "My faith helps me cope with situations. I think it's easy to feel that no child is ever healthy or that something will always go wrong when you're seeing that day in and day out. For me, the realization that God created life and that most of the time things are fine is a perspective that helps me deal with the difficult things I see on a daily basis." She has seen occasions where spiritual practices have helped patients cope, and in those cases, psychosocial aspects of a genetic disorder take a back seat, she says.

She relates two cases of difficult pregnancies

that she remembers well. "One couple had planned a pregnancy and spent a lot of time and energy trying to conceive, then when they did, they discovered there was an age-related chromosome abnormality. Another woman was tested because a genetics screening test was abnormal. In both cases, the women carried babies with chromosomal abnormalities to term, after first praying about their decisions. Continuing a pregnancy or bringing a child into the world with these problems was something they really struggled with. Prayer helped them through the difficult process; they didn't feel alone."

> *"Continuing a pregnancy or bringing a child into the world with these problems was something they really struggled with. Prayer helped them through the difficult process; they didn't feel alone."*

Genetic counseling is very rewarding work, Davidson says, but such work takes its toll on a counselor. Her faith and the intangible rewards are what keep her going. "I feel I'm helping people, but it's taxing emotionally."

A conclusion Davidson might not readily draw, but one which seems fitting, is a connection between the prayers she utters prior to a patient consultation and the "fragrance" that comes from knowing Christ. A psalmist once called upon the Lord to count his prayers as incense before God (Psalm 141: 2) and that plea summons fragrant images to mind.

What Davidson described in terms of praying before meeting with a patient to give her strength for her work parallels the psalmist's plea for God's presence in times of trouble. St. Paul expressed this presence of God in equally pungent terms in his second letter to the the congregation at Corinth. He spoke of spreading the fragrance of knowing Christ in every place, and went on to liken believers to the aroma of Christ in God's presence.

Fragrances are powerful. They can't be seen or felt, but they can sometimes speak to our hearts and sometimes permeate the deepest reaches of our souls, as the psalmist well realized. In inexplicable ways, the aroma of Christ can comfort both a mother who agonizes over the fate of her child and the patient counselor who mirrors for the mother the language of her grief and her hope.

ಬಂಐ

Questions:

1. Have you ever thought of yourself as "the fragrance of Christ?" Do you think the metaphor is fitting? Why or why not?
2. When someone is making a very difficult decision, what do you think is most helpful to them?
3. Davidson sees her role as a counselor to listen and mirror her clients feelings. Why do you think those actions are helpful?
4. Do you think it's appropriate for a genetics counselor to let his or her personal view on abortion or other moral issues affect the counseling they provide? Why or why not?
5. What is the value of praying for someone, when they aren't aware they are being prayed for?

Dr. Katherine Klaassen

Katherine Klaassen received her Doctor of Medicine degree from the University of Kansas School of Medicine. From there, she worked as a Resident in Psychiatry at the Karl Menninger School of Psychiatry in Kansas.

For the past eleven years, Klaassen has worked as a staff psychiatrist for adult and geriatric programs at Utica Psychiatric Services of Hillcrest Healthcare Systems. Since 1994, she has also worked as a Clinical Assistant Professor of Psychiatry with the University of Oklahoma College of Medicine. She is a member of the American Psychiatric Association. Klaassen has given lectures on Alzheimer's and Dementias, Depression in Long-Term Care, Panic Disorder, and Post-Traumatic Stress Disorder. She is a member of the Partners in Mission medical/psychiatric team that is dedicated to providing medical assistance in the impoverished country of Guyana, South America.

Klaassen has been married to her husband, Dan, for fifteen years. Together they have two sons: Chris who is ten, and Stephen, seven. She is a member of Fellowship Lutheran Church in Tulsa, Oklahoma. In her own words, Klaassen tells us, "Faith and family serve as a continued support and staying power in my life."

A Matter of Perspective

ೲ

For everything its season, and for every activity under heaven
its time: a time to be born and a time to die; a time to plant and
a time to uproot; a time to kill and a time to heal; a time to pull
down and a time to build up; a time to weep and a time to laugh;
a time for mourning and a time for dancing; a time to scatter
stones and a time to gather them; a time to embrace and a time to
refrain from embracing; a time to seek and a time to lose; a time
to keep and a time to throw away; a time to tear and a time to
mend; a time for silence and a time for speech; a time to love and
a time to hate; a time for war and a time for peace.
(Ecclesiastes 3: 1-8, NEV)

"We know that when people have made it through our doors, they have usually tried everything else." Kathy Klaassen, M.D., works as an adult and geriatric psychiatrist in Tulsa. She is describing the obstacles her patients face in seeking her help. "Even today, people struggle over whether mental illness is a medical disorder or a character weakness. In another doctor's office people are willing to expose all the body parts we naturally want to hide, and yield them up to be examined by a physician.

97

But when it comes to examining matters of the heart, soul, and mind, they pull away. People are more frightened about having their personalities scrutinized than exposing their naked bodies."

Clearly, Klaassen is frustrated with the way our society views mental health. Jokes continue to be made about "needing professional help." While we don't expect someone to "tough it out" if they suffer from a broken arm or paralyzed limbs, we are not so sure what to do about those suffering from mental illness. Most American adults have had at least one well-meaning relative that advised them to "just get over it," "grow up," or "focus on the positive." Unfortunately, for some, platitudes and positive thinking are just not enough.

> *Most adults have had at least one well-meaning relative that advised them to "just get over it," "grow up," or "focus on the positive." Unfortunately, for some, platitudes and positive thinking are just not enough.*

In the New Testament, the theme of forgiveness comes up numerable times. Yet for some Christians with mental illness, the very act of forgiving seems unfathomable. These are the people who arrive at Klaassen's office saying, "I know I am supposed to forgive them, but I just can't do it!" Klaassen says, "On the one hand, patients realize it is important to forgive those who have hurt them, or at least they acknowledge that society expects forgiveness. On the other hand, you might as well ask them to speak in Greek." She approaches the subject by letting her patients know that she doesn't expect them to forgive. "Once they understand this, they are able to let go of the forgiveness issue and deal with healing and reconciliation in other ways." Next, after weeks or perhaps months of therapy, she works with the patients to get them to try and understand the perpetrator, who may also have been a victim. Klaassen tells us, "I encourage my patients to see the offender in a different perspective. Both the perpetrator and the victim may have been caught in something that was bigger than the both of them. At the same time, I emphasize that what the perpetrator did is not acceptable or excusable."

Humans are social animals. Klaassen says, "Whenever the individuals I see isolate themselves from the community, there is a possibility their problems may worsen." A churchgoer herself, Klaassen experiences firsthand the importance of belonging to a community. She often asks her patients if they are involved in any "clubs, church, or organizations." In this way, she finds out what people do and don't have in their lives. "I am also able to explore the religious dimension, without judgment or threat, when it is lumped in with 'clubs and organizations.' For patients who seem isolated, I encourage them to get involved in something. Often, I suggest finding a church or service group."

Very often, the chronically mentally ill have felt excluded from others in the past. Klaassen explains, "Their differences are just odd enough to make them stand out. When this is the case, I recommend finding a large church or organization where it is easy to blend in and become invisible. What is important is that they become a part of a larger community, while staying within their comfort level."

Sometimes, however, her patients need a little more help. "People suffering from panic disorder may struggle with going to public or crowded places," Klaassen says. "They live in fear of when the next panic attack will arrive. When it does, they experience an 'adrenaline rush'. Their pulse quickens, their palms sweat, and the only thing they want to do is get out of that situation as soon as possible." Because the worship experience occurs in a very public setting, advance planning is needed. Klaassen explains, "People suffering from panic disorder are afraid of experiencing a panic attack in the middle of church. It could happen at any time: during a hymn, at communion, or while the pastor is preaching." For those with panic disorder, Klaassen recommends sitting in a balcony or cry room, where they can slip out unobtrusively. "I work with my patients to look for creative solutions, beyond medications, to improve their quality of life."

In her work, Klaassen has witnessed much suffering due to chronic, terribly debilitating illnesses. Suicide is very high among certain psychiatric illnesses. Watching these people cope with their disease makes her wonder how they manage to be so strong. "I have learned that depression is only temporary, while suicide is permanent. It's all a matter of perspective: you've got to keep your eyes on the big picture."

As she got up to leave, Klaassen commented on my jewelry. "I noticed you are wearing a tortoise. It has become a symbol of hope in my office." For Klaassen, much of her work seems to occur at a turtle's pace. Psychotherapy is long-term work and progress may appear slow and hard to measure. She would love nothing more than to tell a new patient, "take this and tomorrow you'll wake up a new person." Instead, she has to tell them that "in two to four weeks your medications and therapy may help you to feel better." Like the plodding tortoise in the fable, Klaassen has witnessed first hand that "slow and steady" does indeed win the race.

ଈୠଔ

Questions:

1. What is your first instinct, when someone tells you they have decided to seek counseling?
2. Read the description of the two men with demons found in Matthew 8: 28-34. How would these men be looked upon today, in light of the knowledge we have?
3. In our families, we are often confused about how much information to give the children about mental illness or addiction problems within the family. What unspoken messages are sent when the adults in charge neglect to deal with this issue? How does this affect communication within the family?
4. In your opinion, which is worse: to suffer from a life-threatening physical ailment, or a "chronic, debilitating psychiatric illness?"

Rev. David Frerichs

David Frerichs graduated from Wichita State University, Wichita, Kansas with a bachelor's degree in linguistics. At the same institution he later earned a Masters of Education in counseling in 1996. During his years as a graduate student at Wichita State, and after graduation, Frerichs worked there as Program Counselor, Student Support Services. For nine years his work as mentor, support resource coordinator, and academic counselor involved serving first generation college students from low income backgrounds. In 2002 he earned his Master of Divinity from Wartburg Theological Seminary. He is presently pastor of Bethany Lutheran Church in Tulsa, Oklahoma.

The son of a Lutheran pastor, Frerichs grew up in Nebraska and graduated from high school in Kansas. He now lives with his wife, Dawn, and children Daniel, 13, and Megan, 7, in Tulsa, OK. He enjoys riding his mountain bike on excursions with his son, or riding his tandem bike with Dawn or Daniel.

Frerichs enjoys working with people who are on the margins of life, and believes that passion drives him to seek out "those on the edge, and reach out to them." He also enjoys reading "from a wide variety of resources, and particularly appreciates time in the imagined world of a good novel."

Holy Spirit Moments

ഔരു

*"Lord, when was it that we saw you hungry and gave you food,
or thirsty and gave you something to drink? And when was it
that we saw you a stranger and welcomed you, or naked and
gave you clothing? And when was it that we saw you sick or
in prison and visited you?" And the king will answer them,
"Truly, I tell you, just as you did it to one of the least of these
who are members of my family, you did it to me."
(Matthew 25: 37-40)*

David Frerichs didn't want to do what his dad did. Constantly on call. Every holiday a work day. For 18 years he said *"no"* to becoming a minister. When he went off to college he chose to study linguistics. Pretty far from the ministry. Later, when he realized how much he loved working with a unique population at the university, he decided to earn another degree in counseling. And it was that experience of counseling, though productive and rewarding in its own right, which finally led to his experiencing and accepting the call to ordained ministry. A round-about way to becoming a Lutheran pastor, yet it was a path which prepared him well for his eventual vocation. He is presently serving his first parish.

Frerichs can now see the spiritual strands he had even then woven into his counseling sessions. He states that he was technically called an academic counselor, dealing with mostly educational problems and opportunities. He worked with a very special population. The federal government had created and funded an important program called the "TRIO Programs," and he worked under that program in the Student Support Services department for low income and/or physically disabled college students. These students were first generation college students, what Frerichs called "family pioneers." He functioned as their coach, offering them a wholistic approach to education, helping them academically, socially, emotionally, and even spiritually.

But there were also times when his students enriched his own life. Frerichs told the story of a student who from time to time would enter his office, look at his face and say, "You look like you need a song today." Then she, an African-American woman who had been raised Roman Catholic, but had since become a Pentacostal, would stand before him and sing "this wonderful spiritual," and his day would be filled with grace.

Many times he talked with his students about prayer. Mostly it was a sustaining element in their lives, but in some cases it was not what Frerichs would have defined as healthy prayer. He said that one woman continued to make destructive decisions for herself and her family, and she repeatedly blamed those decisions on God, believing that God had directed her to those conclusions during her prayer time. Even then, before studying at the seminary, Frerichs understood that "sometimes we have a tendency to justify our words and actions as God's will." This woman couldn't change her dysfunctional thinking and actions because "something in her system didn't allow her to break free."

Frerichs said that the best parts of counseling were those times when "it all came together." He said at those times it felt as if something bigger was happening, something more than just two people in a room sharing a conversation or solving a problem. Frerichs even came up with a phrase to describe that feeling. He calls them "Holy Spirit moments."

Trying to describe that theological concept in psychological jargon he called it a "gestalt," an understanding that the whole is greater than the sum of the parts, but went on to say that it was still something more than that. It was at the heart of what Frerichs tried to do with those he counseled. He attempted to lead them to more than just an understanding, to lead them, with God's help, into a new vision. He added that he probably would never have been happy doing private practice counseling because it took a long time to get to that point for him. He liked to have time on his side, no rushing, because the pulling together of all the loose threads of a person's life needed to be done gently. He knows that for most counselors time is not granted without limits.

He believed that self-disclosure increased the trust level between them and allowed students to feel safe with him. He felt real compassion for the students.

Frerichs always felt that he was open to any of the students' problems. Because he was not judgmental, and he would disclose parts of his own life experience with students, they responded well to him. He believed that self-disclosure increased the trust level between them and allowed students to feel safe with him. He felt real compassion for the students. The word "compassion," meaning "to suffer along with," is a concept he uses in the ministry as well. He fought the changing governmental regulations that "yanked funds from our students." He also sided with students when his administrators wanted him to spend less time with students and more time in bureaucratic paperwork. "Holy Spirit moments" took time to develop, and Frerichs did not want to shortchange his students.

Frerichs remembers only two occasions in his graduate program in counseling when professors spoke about spirituality and counseling. The first occured when a faculty member, who had attended divinity school, warned all of the students before taking the comprehensive examinations that they should not use theological language. He explained that the theological and anthropological explanations in the church used different vocabulary from psychology and counseling. "Do not use the term 'brokenness,' which is a theological concept," he warned. He said they could use those terms in their own faith life, but not in their professional life. That dichotomy puzzled Frerichs and he approached his own pastor with the dilemma. His pastor's reply was not helpful. He merely said, "I'm sure you'll work it out." Frerichs has worked it out, but he regrets that more discussion of spiritual issues were not included in his training.

The second time the topic was addressed it was in an ethics class. The question was: Is it necessary to disclose your own religious background before counseling with someone? One of the students in the class, a fundamentalist Christian, stated that she had an ethical responsibility to declare her position on such issues as abortion, divorce etc. However, the professor, a Gestalt therapist whom Frerichs described as "full of grace," responded by telling the students that "it was important to be clear, and that you may have to say it later, but you should not start the conversation by declaring your side."

During those early years Frerichs also volunteered as a youth crisis counselor at National Lutheran Youth Gatherings. Here, more than anywhere else, Frerichs felt as though he represented (re- presented) Christ in the moment. He worked with groups of adolescents and their adult sponsors who were having trouble communicating. He didn't stop his interventions with them until they could talk to one another again with civility and love. He felt that he became the vehicle through which Christ worked.

Frerichs always kept the "Christ question," in mind, that is: "What is it I can do for you?" "Too often," he said, "we decide what people need before we engage in a meaningful relationship with that person." Frerichs believes that what Jesus taught us in the Bible, to care for others, is a great mission. It was during one of those youth gatherings when his supervisor first asked Frerichs if he had ever thought about entering the ministry.

Frerichs recalls that the "Christ question," what he calls "the core of my theology," was even on his mind when he wrote his developmental psychology paper in graduate school. As he looks back he realizes he was always spiritual, specifically Christian and Lutheran, in his counseling, even though he made it a point to listen carefully to and respect the values and beliefs of others. Frerichs believes that being present in the moment really means representing Christ in the moment, with all the power and responsibility that statement holds. Whether as a counselor, a pastor, a parishioner, a friend, Frerichs will say in the spirit of Jesus, "What is it I can do for you?"

ഗ‍ര

Questions:

1. What is the "Christ Question" and how does it apply to the client/therapist relationship? How does it apply to your life?

2. Who in our society could be considered "one of the least of these?" Who are the unseen, the un-heard, the un-touched of your church, your community, your state, your country, your world? Do you or your church family have a ministry to them?

3. What does Frerichs mean by the term "Holy Spirit moment?" Have you ever experienced one? When? Did it change your feelings or behavior?

4. What does it mean to be a "family pioneer?" In what ways can we be Christian pioneers in the twenty-first century.

5. Discuss "healthy prayer." How do we know when it becomes unhealthy?

6. What is the difference between "sympathy" and "empathy?" Which is truer "compassion," meaning "to suffer along with"? What does Jesus ask of us? Is absolute honesty always compassionate?

Dr. Erwin Janssen

Erwin Janssen received his M.D. from the University of Iowa in 1962. From 1962 until his retirement in 1999 as Vice President/Chief of Psychiatry for Children's Medical Center in Tulsa, Oklahoma, Janssen practiced psychiatry with mostly pediatric patients. After service in the U.S. Navy, Janssen spent much of his career at the Menninger Clinic in Topeka, Kansas, where he was on staff from 1968 until 1992. Currently, he consults part-time with the Columbia Valley Community Health Clinic in Wenatchee, Washington and as a consultant to private practitioners.

Janssen's civic and professional activities have been numerous and diverse, including service within various local church congregations, service to residential facilities for the developmentally disabled, and dozens of appointments or elections to medical professional boards and organizations. He is currently active in music ministry programs at Fellowship Lutheran Church in Tulsa. Janssen and his wife Maurine have two grown daughters, both of whom are also psychiatrists.

As a result of ongoing interest in medical and mental health issues globally, Janssen coordinates mission work in Guyana, South America, through a program called Partners in Mission. Janssen spearheaded the program in 1996, which has supported the work of more than 100 professional and lay volunteers from all over the U.S., who have participated in mission projects that have included medical and/or dental clinics, education seminars, music education, youth programs, construction projects, mental health support, sewing instruction, and computer education. Janssen has personally traveled to Guyana to coordinate such projects about twenty times in the past seven years.

Good Fruits

ℰℐℭℛ

"Who is wise and understanding among you? Show by your good life that your works are done with gentleness born of wisdom . . . But the wisdom from above is first pure, then peaceable, gentle, willing to yield, full of mercy and good fruits, without a trace of partiality or hypocrisy. And a harvest of righteousness is sown in peace for those who make peace." (James 3: 13, 17 - 18)

It's one thing to recognize that citizens of a third-world country—the second poorest in the western hemisphere—have few mental health resources. It's another thing entirely to look into the face of a psychiatric patient in Guyana, South America and see a man without hope.

"Fort Canje National Psychiatric Hospital is the only mental hospital serving the country, and conditions there are deplorable," says psychiatrist Dr. Erwin "Erv" Janssen. He first visited Guyana in 1996, as part of a medical mission team from Fellowship Lutheran Church in Tulsa. "In the U.S. we regularly place mental health activities very low in our priorities and I had already seen the physical evidence of difficult years in Guyana, so I should not have been surprised at what I saw," Janssen says.

"Buildings were deteriorated, most of them abandoned because they were unsafe. There were piles of rubble, overgrowth of vegetation, split and stained mattresses without sheets. The effects of the elements— intense sun, termites and rain in a rain forest country— along with the years of neglect, were evident. There were holes in office floors, little furniture, steps missing, and no railings. More disturbing, the empty facial features of those with whom we talked gave testimony to discouragement and a sense of helplessness and hopelessness. In spite of all of this, the staff tried to care for patients with the few medications available. As I remember, they had two psychiatrists for around 200 patients. We were told many patients were left at the facility by families who pretend they no longer exist."

The visit to Fort Canje was not a primary focus of the 1996 mission trip, which was coordinated by Janssen to provide medical clinics in parishes of the Lutheran Church in Guyana, or LCG. One of the LCG pastors arranged the Fort Canje trip at Janssen's request to satisfy his curiosity about the country's mental health services. What the mission team saw there was dispiriting.

"It was more personal seeing their faces," Janssen says, as opposed to thinking of needs in a theoretical sense. "Given the dire straits of the hospital and its patients, I recognized the uphill struggle, the demoralization and helplessness people felt. There seemed to be an opportunity for future mission teams to reach beyond the LCG and allow them to bring hope into their communities." The Partners in Mission ministry project was undertaken to supply not only physical and medical needs, but also spiritual encouragement to the people of Guyana. "Hopelessness is pervasive, and we wanted to stimulate and elevate hope," Janssen says.

In the years that followed, the Partners in Mission ministry expanded far beyond what Janssen first envisioned. Mission teams—which have now included more than a hundred people from all over the U.S.—and which make the trip to South America several times a year, have undertaken such projects as music and sewing instruction, building construction or renovation, medical and dental clinics, computer classes and support, educational programs for physicians, youth programs, and public teacher training clinics. They now serve not only individual Lutheran congregations and clergy, but the Evangelical Lutheran Church in Guyana (ELCG, as the national church is now called), as well as the communities to which ELCG churches minister. During each mission trip to Guyana, Janssen devotes at least some energy to providing resource material or training to psychiatric workers and clinicians. His enthusiasm for this work inspires others to give of themselves as well.

Of this incredible falling-in-place of resources, Janssen says simply, "The good Lord seems to guide."

Individuals or organizational representatives have stepped forward from often surprising places and in unexpected ways to assist mission projects, offering everything from financial assistance or donation of critical supplies or medications, to networking contact names and offers to volunteer time and talent in Guyana. Of this incredible falling-in-place of resources, Janssen says simply, "The good Lord seems to guide."

These words hint at a profound faith that infuses both his professional and personal activities with compassion. Janssen is very clear, however, about the difference between his responsibilities as a physician and his responsibilities as a Christian. He recognizes that people live according to their beliefs, but often without stating them. "I couldn't ever in good conscience suggest substituting prayer for medical treatment to a patient," he says. There have been occasions during Janssen's career, in fact, when parents have rejected standard pharmacological therapies for their children in favor of relying on prayer alone for healing. "I have had to ensure that such situations are reported to the authorities."

That's not to say Janssen doesn't recognize the value of faith or prayer in a patient's healing. "Prayer is a part of personal and family process and is important, but in treating psychological components with a biological basis, to *not* use available medical treatments would be a shame. Rather, it would be malpractice." When a patient or family member expresses the need for spiritual support, Janssen is eager to recommend consulting with a hospital chaplain or other clergy.

As a physician, Janssen recognizes the vulnerability of patients he treats and believes that to attempt to influence their religious beliefs would be abuse. "A patient doesn't come to me for prayer," he says, "and a psychiatrist doesn't have to be a Christian to be competent technically. He or she must remain objective. I don't use my position or time with patients to proselytize."

Most of Janssen's career was spent working with pediatric patients. "Working with kids is a way of preventing serious problems later in their lives. It's a tragedy in Oklahoma that people aren't interested enough in kids to see they have the resources to grow into healthy adults. Children have a God-given resiliency that often prevails, even when provided with only 'good enough' parenting," he says, but he's discouraged by how often even that is lacking.

Also lacking is adequate psychiatric or psychological services for children and adolescents, particularly in rural areas. "There aren't enough, even in Tulsa," Janssen says. "More psychotropic medications are prescribed by internists and pediatricians than by psychiatrists. Some childhood depression resolves on its own, but most cases need intervention. The best approach is usually psychotherapy plus medication, and most youngsters don't get either." He thinks an inadequate number of practitioners is partly to blame. Economics is another major factor: state services are usually provided from a short-sighted mentality, in his view, without concern for the long run.

Janssen believes that attending to young people's emotional and developmental needs, when seen from a philosophical-theological perspective, is a stewardship issue. "I like to think it allows them to maximize their skills, personal resources, and potential."

In addition to his work in South America, Janssen volunteers his professional expertise at a medical clinic for children of migrant workers in Wenatchee, Washington four weeks a year. Unfortunately, in this capacity Janssen sees many children with little opportunity to reach their potential. Many of his patients' parents don't speak English. Janssen makes use of an interpreter in those cases.

"Each clinical setting is a different population. These children, whose ages range from two to fourteen, live in families where drugs, poverty, abuse, and neglect are an added burden for the children. There are a lot of Attention Deficit Hyperactivity Disorder (ADHD) or mood disorder diagnoses; some post-traumatic stress disorders. Medications are helpful, but the Children's Home Society in Washington is also helpful with providing therapy. Most of these families subsist on welfare, and it's hard to keep a clinical practice going if the only patients are poor," he says, but he sees the work there as vital. In situations like this, Janssen says a sensitive public school system can be a critical ally.

He relates the story of a fourteen-year-old boy with a reading disability whose mother, also suffering from a reading disability, did not want her son in special education. "The mother had unpleasant experiences with special education twenty years before. The boy had a high enough IQ, but was high risk and was severely depressed with low self-esteem and hopelessness. He couldn't read. Prescribing antidepressants alone couldn't solve the problem."

The longer such students go without help, Janssen says, the more difficult it becomes for them academically and emotionally. Schools that are willing to step in and provide resources in a positive atmosphere can contribute to overall success. In times of economic stress, schools simply haven't got the resources, though, he says, and parents are left with few options. "So often parents can't understand the system and just give up. They're demoralized by the time I see them." This is where the church can also play a role, Janssen says. He stresses the importance of church youth programs to keep young people connected to a community where problems might be detected and where support and encouragement is available. The value of such communities isn't always visible, however. "It's hard to study the effects of prayer, because the Holy Spirit isn't scientifically measurable."

"It's hard to study the effects of prayer, because the Holy Spirit isn't scientifically measurable."

Another area where Janssen proceeds with caution is in defining what patients or family members mean when using terms that imply spirituality. "Some patients insist on a Christian clinician because they want to know they won't be made fun of. Others want to be sure the physician has the same beliefs they do." In either case, Janssen believes it's not helpful to make too many assumptions about what is meant when using the words "spirituality" or "Christian." When dealing with young patients, Janssen thinks it's also important to understand that belief systems aren't yet fully evolved.

Karl Menninger, who helped establish the Menninger Clinic in Topeka, Kansas where Janssen was trained, was insistent on understanding the development of human spirituality. "We had visiting speakers and theologians when I was a resident who spoke on the topic," Janssen says. "I had also read some work about it." Otherwise, his medical training—as appears to be the norm, then and now—said little about integrating faith and health. As a result, Janssen preserves a separation between his personal beliefs and his professional practices. "Your values go along with you," he says, "but you honor your patients' own belief systems. You don't use your clinical or administrative position to influence either your patients or your colleagues."

In fact, Janssen says that some of his colleagues may not be aware that he is Lutheran or Christian. His Christian values, however, affect his perspective on the value and meaning of life, and he thinks those are evident in his practice among children and adolescents.

Those values drive Janssen in his pursuit of shoring up mental health services on two American continents. While his work in Washington allows him to care directly for patients, his role in Guyana is one of building up mental health professionals through educational programs, encouragement, and tangible resources such as videos and textbooks. "A gentleman who often drives me while I'm in Guyana noted that I had brought videos on several occasions. He said one day, 'You know, they don't have a VCR there.' They had received the videos I'd brought gratefully each time, but they were reluctant to tell me they didn't have a VCR," Janssen explains. He secured one and delivered it during a subsequent trip.

Janssen's concern led him recently to locate a former medical director of the Ft. Canje hospital. "In the mid-sixties, Forbes Burnham was ushered in as President of Guyana, and whose style of leadership proved very difficult for Guyana and the Guyanese people. At the same time, the medical director was ushered out by Burnham's personal choice for the same position. I found him in Florida. Though he is quite elderly and has suffered a stroke, he was kind enough to send me papers relating to the hospital at the time he left. Apparently, it was once a 'Jewel of the Caribbean' in terms of mental health," Janssen says. "It was years ahead of many state hospital programs in the U.S. at the time. In Guyana, they saw the community as part of the treatment program," he adds, in sharp contrast to the condition of treatment programs in Guyana at present.

Janssen's Christian values also lead him to supply whatever needs he discovers, wherever he finds himself. "We were down in 2001 with a mental health team," Janssen says, "and the workers were so eager to see us. They often deal with patients who are aggressive and difficult to manage, particularly without adequate medications available. They asked for help with managing those patients."

In characteristic fashion, Janssen researched and located in the U.S. the creator of a training program aimed at teaching mental health workers to control aggressive patients. "Lo and behold, David Mandt of Dallas, who founded the Mandt System for training hospitals to deal with aggressive patients, volunteered to go to Guyana with our mission team in October of 2002 and again in 2003 and 2004 to begin a series of courses to train a core group of about a dozen mental health workers in his system. He plans to continue going, at his own expense, until the group is fully trained to train others in the method. In that way, they become self-sustaining."

It's this sort of blessed coincidence that seems to accompany Janssen's many journeys in Christian service. He shrugs and speaks of the wonders of the Holy Spirit, as though it accompanies his ministry but not his professional practice. The writer of the book of James speaks of the good fruits of a good life, one in which works are done with gentleness born of wisdom, without partiality or hypocrisy.

Perhaps there are times when such gentle wisdom is an instrument of the Holy Spirit, even when the spirit is not named. Perhaps when a man is infused with the power of the Holy Spirit, everything he does is touched by the same Spirit.

ഇൗര

Questions:

1. What do you think James meant by "gentleness born of wisdom?"
2. What are the "good fruits" of the kind of life James describes?
3. Why do you think it's important that Dr. Janssen is careful not to let his personal beliefs encroach on his treatment of patients?
4. Do you think it's possible to compartmentalize our spiritual faith, separate from our professional or civic lives? In what ways do they interact?
5. How does the status of your spiritual journey change the way you behave professionally or in community with your neighbors?

Dr. Edward Decker

Edward Decker began his professional life in Hawaii, where he worked as a pastor of two Assembly of God churches. He holds two M.S. degrees in Counseling Psychology and in Administration and Organizational Behavior. In 1987, he graduated with a Ph.D. in Educational Psychology from Kent State University.

Since 1988, Decker has served as a Professor of Christian Counseling and a Coordinator of Graduate Programs in Counseling at Oral Roberts University School of Theology & Missions. In 1990, he successfully launched a private counseling practice in Tulsa. Decker and his wife, Terese Hall, work as Directors of Pastoral Care and Counseling at Fellowship Lutheran Church in Tulsa, Oklahoma, where he is also a member.

Throughout Decker's career, he has been actively involved in consulting work for numerous groups as diverse as the National Dairy Administration and the National Association of Legal Assistants. He is widely published, having written articles for *Catholic Digest* and *Christian Counseling Today*, as well as other publications. In 1998, Decker presented an article entitled "Does the Holy Spirit Really Make a Difference in Therapy?" for the Fellowship of Pentecostal-Charismatic Caregivers Website Symposium.

Decker enjoys a rewarding career in a fascinating field. He shares his adventures with his wife, Terese, children Dave, Dawn and her husband David, plus two grandchildren. When he is not working, he can often be found in the garden.

Divine Human Encounters

When I look up at thy heavens, the work of thy fingers, the moon and the stars set in their place by thee, what is man that thou shouldst remember him, mortal man that thou shouldst care for him? Yet thou hast made him little less than a god, crowning him with glory and honour. Thou makest him master over all thy creatures; thou hast put everything under his feet...(Psalms 8: 3-6, NEB)

ॐ

When Dr. Ed Decker first began marital counseling in 1975, many within the church that he sprang from shunned the idea of counseling. The son of two ordained missionaries in the Hawaiian Islands, Decker has been a part of the Pentecostal/Charismatic community all his life. He has spent his career as an educator and counselor promoting the belief that a health professional's Christian faith can be combined with psychological therapy to encourage healing. Decker has witnessed much progress in this area over the last twenty-nine years. Today, the schools of psychology and counseling are met with wide acceptance at Oral Roberts University, where Decker works as a professor of Christian Counseling.

When speaking with other counseling professionals, Decker continues to fight for a marriage of faith and counseling principles. He struggles with his peers to gain acceptance for his belief that one's faith in God permeates the health professional's work in a positive way. Like everyone else in the field, Decker was taught to keep his religious views separate from his professional life. On the other hand, he tells us, "Clients have every right to ask for a Christian counselor. Research, in fact, has born out that people want to see people that are like them. But there is a lot of confusion over what the term 'Christian counselor' actually means. For instance, some counselors are Christian, but their faith may or may not show itself in their practice. For others in the field, the term 'Christian counseling' actually means biblical counseling. The definition I use demands that the principles applied in counseling flow out of the ethics of Jesus; the ethics of love, justice, and mercy."

For the last twenty-seven years, Decker has been teaching and leading seminars on the integration of faith and counseling. Here, he describes four guiding principles that have given shape to his own counseling practice. "First, there exists a worldview that is oriented toward the Christian faith. Second, the goals of Christian counseling may differ from non-Christian counseling. Third, the Christian counselor uses a variety of techniques to establish legal, moral, and ethical boundaries to his/her practice. For instance, everything said or done should be consistent with God's Word. Fourth, this counselor ministers to a unique subculture: the people of God."

However, there is much about the practice of counseling that cannot be described in words, or contained in a textbook. The best counseling always depends on individualizing the therapy to fit the situation. Decker tells us, "There is no *carte blanche* in this business. You cannot pull out a list of questions and fire them off at the client. One, two, three, and you are healed. It takes time, listening skills and an intuitive sense to prescribe the right treatment for each person that walks through the door."

To that end, Decker readily relies on the empowerment of the Holy Spirit during counseling sessions. He instructs his divinity students to be aware of the ways in which the Holy Spirit guides the counselor. In his classes at the university, Decker describes five ways in which the Spirit leads Christian counselors in their work. First, there is Knowledge: the comprehension of God's word. Second, there is Revelation: God reveals things to you that you wouldn't normally know. Third is Discernment: which includes insight into the real problem. Fourth, there is Illumination: the shining moment when things begin to make sense. Finally, there is Wisdom: the knowing how to do it and when to do it. All of this utilizes the training and experience of the counselor in what Decker calls, "a divine human encounter".

When asked what has been a guiding principle in his ministry, Decker speaks of the compassion he feels for people. "I want to help them be more than they can be by themselves." He continues by sharing a quote from Chancellor Roberts, founder of ORU: "With the grace of God and by the empowerment of the Holy Spirit, we help people get better."

As people of God, we are called to live our lives in a way that reflects the love of God. Oftentimes, this decision to live out our faith throws us into direct conflict with the world. Most mental health professionals are called upon to operate with indifference to God, in their professional lives. How does this affect Decker and his colleagues, who actively promote the importance of integrating the Christian experience with the practice of counseling? With the confidence of a seasoned pilgrim Decker concludes, "Whatever happens next, it will be fine. Believing in spite of what I see, and in spite of what I know, I trust God."

ഔര

Questions:

1. How does your faith in God carry over into your professional life?
2. In Biblical times, it was considered normal that whole nations would believe in the same god, whether it was Jehovah, or Allah, or Shiva. Today, it is increasingly common to have many faiths represented within the same political boundary. What consequences has this change had on our society?
3. Would you feel threatened, if you were called upon to pray with a fellow co-worker? Would you pray inside your place of employment, or outside?

Judith Mayton

Judith Mayton holds degrees from the University of Southern Mississippi and Northeastern State University. She began her career as an English teacher, where she says she felt drawn to the students with special challenges. For 20 years she has worked in the area of pastoral counseling. Mayton is an experienced marriage and family therapist, as well. She is a member of the Christian Association for Psychological Studies (CAPS).

Mayton has 16 years of experience working as a college professor, which is decidedly her first love. Oral Roberts University is where she is currently employed as a Professor of Behavioral Sciences.

Mayton and her husband reside in Tulsa. She is a member of Fellowship Lutheran Church, where she is very active in the music program, both as a member of the choir and as an accompanist. She is a mother, grandmother, and a good friend to many. In her spare time, she enjoys tending her flower beds.

Created for a Purpose

ഇൗ

*For it is by his grace you are saved, through trusting him; it
is not your own doing. It is God's gift, not a reward for work
done. There is nothing for anyone to boast of. For we are God's
handiwork, created in Christ Jesus to devote ourselves to the
good deeds for which God has designed us. (Ephesians 2: 8-10)*

No matter what one's calling in life, there is
a natural tendency for each of us to behave
as if success or bitter failure depends solely
upon our individual efforts. However, deep down, we
realize our control over our world is only an illusion. In
the time it takes to swallow, a car accident could strip us of
everything that is dear to us, including our very lives. For
the Christian, learning to accept God's will for our lives is
often in direct conflict with our natural desire to care for
ourselves and those we love.

Dr. Judith Mayton has for many years been helping
other Christians in crisis sort out their own unique location
in the kingdom of God. The only child of an Assembly
of God minister, she grew up visiting members in their
homes or in the hospital with her father. Mayton tells us,

"I learned many of the skills I use as a therapist today from my father. Nearly every day, I witnessed him presenting the gospel of Jesus Christ with his own unique person. He always taught that Jesus is always accessible." Today she acknowledges the impact that time had on her, and what a blessing those memories have become.

"I feel as called to my work as my husband, who is a minister, does to his." She also sees a limited number of people for counseling; usually, a church refers these people to Mayton. "In my therapy work I have made it a point to stay away from the label 'Christian counselor.' I feel this term has limiting connotations associated with it. It says I cannot deal with non-Christians. Instead, I refer to myself as a passionate follower of Jesus Christ who is also a therapist."

Mayton's personal preparation for a counseling session always includes a time for solitary prayer. "I ask the Holy Spirit to reveal the mind of Christ to us. I pray for insight, and for patience. I pray that the Holy Spirit will walk with them, and walk with me, so neither of us will back off from the 'lancing of the wound' that needs to take place. The apostle Paul refers to 'speaking the truth in love' in his epistle to the Ephesians. There is no substitute for looking at what really exists in our lives, if we are to overcome it. It takes courage, and that is exactly what I hope to provide for my clients."

When Mayton was asked if she had ever witnessed the Holy Spirit at work in her career, she responded with, "All the time! So much of my therapy experience has been conducted in a Christian setting. I am thankful, because that's just who I am."

There are several personality characteristics that Mayton has come to rely upon in her role as therapist/teacher. "First, I am comfortable with who I am," Mayton says. "I understand I am not perfect. I don't expect others to be perfect, either. Second, God has blessed me with a natural strength, and for that I am thankful. I am thankful for those who have gone before me, and I have learned the importance of a sense of humor." Finally, she adds this: "Even though I haven't always liked this about myself, I would have to include my ability to feel another's pain."

Painful as this ability is, it also serves a purpose. There is one woman who sticks in Mayton's mind, whom she felt a great deal of empathy for. Pam (not her real name) was in her mid-forties when she first met Mayton. A successful businesswoman in the lucrative computers industry, Pam first contacted Mayton because she was confused and hurt by her home situation. "Pam suffered from little to no self-esteem. She had been constantly told she was no good. Furthermore, she had led a promiscuous lifestyle for so long that she could no longer remember all the men she had had sexual relations with. She had two sons, each of them having a different father. At the time of our meeting, she was then married to another man that had three kids of his own, of whom he had custody.

> *"I realized I had to help her with her perception of herself, before any progress could be made in her relationship to others. So I explored with her the nature of Christ."*

"Pam came to me because she was experiencing horrible problems with her marriage. A lot of this had to do with her low esteem, which created jealousy in her heart towards her husband. On the other side, her husband didn't really know how to be married. He believed that family life should revolve around the male authority figure. He was at the center of his universe.

"Pam was a Christian. She felt she was a bad person because of her adulterous past. I realized I had to help her with her perception of herself, before any progress could be made in her relationships to others. So I explored with her the nature of Christ. I used all the therapeutic skills I had to help her accept the forgiveness Christ offers. I pointed out that once we are forgiven,

Christ sees us as perfect and whole. At long last, she realized she was just as pure, as clean and as valuable to her Savior as I was. We were then able to begin the process of family therapy."

Surely, Jesus Christ has enriched the life of Judith Mayton. She has found her safe harbor, her resting-place. But how does Mayton's being a Christian make her better at what she does? "For me personally, I realize there's only one Messiah, and I am not he. Knowing that keeps me from being expected to have all the right answers. It keeps me honest therapeutically. I realize there are some counselors that are better at this or that than me. For instance, while I have done much family counseling, I am not especially gifted with small children. If another professional is better suited to help a client, then they need to know that. You have to know your gifts.

"Christ set us a very good example. Because of that example, I understand the serving part. The act of counseling others cannot become a power trip, if I am to help people where they are."

ഌരു

Questions:

1. Think about your life, and then think about what you do with it. How has God uniquely created you for this work?
2. Was there ever a time in your life when you 'let go and let God' help you with a problem? Were you able to relinquish control?
3. Count your blessings. See if you can come up with a list of fifteen. Share one or two with your group members.

Interview Questions:

1. Do you pray with your patients/clients? Do your patients/clients ever pray for you?
2. Do you feel the presence of God when you see patients/clients? How do you know?
3. Does being a Christian/Lutheran make you different in your practice? How?
4. Do you think patients/clients respond differently to you if or when they know you are a Christian/Lutheran? Do you tell patients/clients? Do they ever ask?
5. Do you believe spiritual, emotional and mental processes interact? How?
6. Have you ever had a patient/client whose religious beliefs contributed to his/her illness or kept them from being healed? Any patient/client whose spirituality helped them to heal? Could you tell us about that?
7. Is there anything you would not do in your practice because you are a Christian/Lutheran?
8. Was there anything in your training that taught you to deal with the spiritual aspects of healing?
9. Was there anything in your church life that helped you deal with the spiritual aspects of healing?
10. Do you have any stories about spirituality and healing in patients/clients with mental health issues?

৪০০৪

From left: Cynthia Gustavson, Janice Airhart (seated), Michele Fox, Linda Holeman, and Patti Schmigle.

About Fellowship, Ink

Fellowship, Ink was formed late in 2002 as a result of Fellowship member Cynthia Gustavson's realization that the Tulsa, Oklahoma congregation's membership includes many mental health professionals. The project was begun as a means to lift up those practitioners in this congregation and others in area ELCA congregations who use their gifts in this way, and to examine the link between emotional healing and spirituality. Group members—all members of Fellowship Lutheran—are:

Janice Airhart was a medical technologist for more than twenty years before obtaining a graduate degree in journalism from the University of Oklahoma in 1994. Since then, she has written two novels and published several articles in local, regional, and national publications, including *Oklahoma Today, New Moon: A Magazine for Girls and Their Dreams, The Lutheran* and *Lutheran Woman Today.* She is a member of the National Association of Science Writers and currently writes and edits two newsletters for The University of Tulsa College of Engineering and Natural Sciences. Airhart and her husband own and operate a marketing center in Tulsa.

Writer *Michele Fox* has only recently embarked on her artistic career. She completed work for a bachelor's degree in elementary education at Texas Lutheran University and the University of Dubuque. Since then, Fox has devoted the last twenty years to working with children in various Lutheran churches, day care facilities, and public schools, where she enjoys helping children explore their sense of fun through artistic play. She resides in Tulsa, Oklahoma, with her pastor husband and three sons and is currently at work on a novel.

Cynthia Gustavson attended Gustavus Adolphus College, graduated from Boston University and Louisiana State University and did further graduate work at United Seminary of the Twin Cities and Oklahoma State University. Gustavson is currently a pastoral counselor at the Center for Counseling and Education in Tulsa, OK. She is the author of *Scents of Place: Seasons of the St. Croix Valley* (Country Messenger Press, Marine on St. Croix, MN., 1987) and *In-Versing Your Life: A Poetry Workbook for Self-Discovery and Healing,* (Families International, Inc., Milwaukee, WI., 1995.) Her poetry, short stories, and articles have appeared in national and regional journals including *The Christian Century, Sojourners, Lutheran Woman Today, The Journal of Poetry Therapy,* and *Families in Society.* Gustavson and her husband live in Tulsa.

Linda Holeman has been a professional writer and editor and currently works as Marketing Communications Manager of a Tulsa telecommunications company. A sometime poet, Holeman's work has appeared in *RDH*, *Proofs*, and *The Legacy*. She holds a B.A. from Texas A&M University and lives with her husband, son, and daughter in Tulsa, Oklahoma.

Patti Schmigle spent 22 years in the energy and communications industries, serving in various technical, management and executive roles. She graduated from Oklahoma State University with a Bachelor of Science degree and obtained her Master of Business Administration from Rockhurst in Kansas City. After leaving her position as vice president of business development for a communications company in Tulsa, Schmigle has turned her sights to writing. This is Schmigle's first non-fiction writing endeavor, but she is working on her first novel. Schmigle lives with her husband and two sons in Tulsa, and serves on the Board of Riverfield Country Day School. She is Executive Director of a nonprofit organization called *Up With Trees*.

$$\wp\mathcal{C}$$

Fellowship, Ink may be contacted through the Fellowship Lutheran church web site: www.flctulsa.org.